God Blessed Our Arms with Victory

God Blessed Our Arms with Victory

The Religious Life of Stonewall Jackson

Warren J. Richards

VANTAGE PRESS
New York / Washington / Atlanta
Los Angeles / Chicago

Copyright © 1986 by Warren J. Richards

Published by Vantage Press, Inc.
516 West 34th Street, New York, New York 10001

Manufactured in the United States of America
ISBN: 0-533-06149-0

Library of Congress Catalog Card No.: 84-90063

To my dyke,
K. R. Wilson

Contents

Foreword

The military genius of Confederate General Thomas Jonathan "Stonewall" Jackson has sometimes been overlooked because of the emphasis writers have placed upon his many eccentricities and religious fundamentalism. However, the key to understanding this unusual man was his Christianity. A deep and abiding faith in Jesus Christ and a belief in the sovereignty of God gave unity and meaning to his life both on and off the battlefield. In fact, he seldom spoke solely in the context of military matters. Instead, he spoke most frequently as a Christian.

After his fervent prayers had failed to delay war, Jackson accepted the conflict as being the will of God. The only course of action left, as he saw it, was to end the struggle as quickly as possible, a conviction that, in some respects, turned him into an extremely stern, iron-willed military commander.

Before and during battle General Jackson prayed frequently, and he always gave his Maker credit for victory. Before Fredericksburg in December, 1862, he remarked to a subordinate: "I trust our God will give us a great victory today, captain." Even on his deathbed following Chancellorsville, Jackson chided General Lee for giving him too much credit for the success of the hour. The glory, he said, should go to God.

Jackson, a Protestant and staunch Calvinistic Presbyterian, did not join the church of his choice until November, 1851, several months after resigning from the United States Army to accept a position on the faculty of the Virginia Military Institute in Lexington, Virginia. But for the next ten years it would have been difficult to find anyone in the Lexington Presbyterian Church who prayed so frequently, disciplined himself more strictly, or attempted to obey the will of God more conscientiously than Professor Jackson.

While a cadet at the Virginia Military Institute, Warren Richards became seriously interested in the famed Confederate general, and the result, some twenty years later, is this informative volume. *God Blessed Our Arms with Victory* provides insights into the character of one of this country's most distinguished military figures. A number of readers, of course, will quibble over parts of the story, but no one should question the necessity and wisdom of viewing Jackson primarily through his religion. A member of the General's staff reached this conclusion over a century ago: "The religion of Stonewall Jackson will be the chief and most effective way into the secret springs of the character and career of this strange man."

John G. Barrett

God Blessed Our Arms
with Victory

CHAPTER ONE

Introduction

*The consciousness of men developes hypocracy, Jesus'
abomination.*

William S. White

It was a pleasant morning in the Old Dominion village of
Lexington. Squirrels were racing across the grass and up the
trees, providing continuous entertainment for the passerby.
The hour was eleven o'clock, and the sun was beginning to
burst through the white mist. Many residents were out for a
walk, enjoying the shade of the towering trees and the scenery
provided by the area. The small, quiet town seemed to be a
nearly perfect place in which to live.

Every morning at this exact hour a peculiar professor
from Lexington's Virginia Military Institute would trudge
through the town on his way home.[1] His huge feet made
walking oddly noticeable.[2] The old fool, Tom Jackson, was
caught up in deep thought and completely detached from the
surroundings. His face portrayed that of a stern and rather
sad man. No one in Lexington really knew him because he
was always quiet and reserved, but everyone knew of him.
Stories and jokes about Jackson were as plentiful as the leaves
on the trees.

1

The superintendent at the Institute had a story about the professor that he told to many of his friends and associates.[3] Each week the major would report to the colonel about his activities. The superintendent noticed that the professor was extremely conscientious about the time and would walk back and forth in front of the superintendent's quarters until the exact hour had arrived to report.[4] One day there was a heavy rainstorm during the afternoon on which Major Jackson was to visit the colonel. Not really expecting the professor to come on such a rainy day, the superintendent looked out his window and to his surprise saw Jackson pacing back and forth in front of his home in the heavy rain. According to Jackson, "the hour had not quite arrived when it was his duty to present the weekly reports."[5] This peculiar man was the most conscientious person that the superintendent had ever met.

The commandant at the Institute also had a story about the professor and his devotion to duty. One day the colonel ordered the major to report to him at a specific time in the late afternoon. The commandant forgot about the appointment, but of course the professor did not and was at the office at the exact hour. When the senior officer returned to the Institute the next morning he found Jackson "sitting straight as a ramrod"[6] and waiting for him. Jackson had been there all night anticipating the arrival of his forgetful superior. [7] Naturally the commandant felt that this type of devotion was approaching the limits of absurdity.

Major Jackson was a frequent topic of conversation among the professors at the Institute. Their humorous gossip was highlighted with a story about the major and his uniform. [8] During the hot, humid days of one summer all of the teachers were wearing the lightest possible uniform, except Jackson. He continued to wear his thick woolen winter uniform. One of his peers asked him why he did not change to the summer uniform, and he replied that "he had seen an order prescribing the uniform which he wore, but none had been exhibited to him directing it to be changed." [9] Most of the officers got a good laugh from this story about Jackson's exact obedience to orders.

According to the citizens of Lexington, the professor was also a religious fanatic.[10] Associated with this fanaticism was a great concern for honesty. Late one night during a rainstorm, Jackson, walking several miles from home, was seen by a friend. After a short conversation, the friend learned that Jackson had informed a fellow professor incorrectly about an interview with a cadet. His friend then asked if it was really necessary to correct the misunderstanding that night and Jackson replied, "I have discovered it was a misstatement and could not sleep comfortably tonight unless I corrected it." [11] Stories such as this swept across the small town like a brush fire.

Jackson was about the oddest character that the people in Lexington had ever seen. He was so conscientious about every detail that it was amusing just to be around him. His devotion to duty was so extreme that people could not identify with the man. Every order was followed to the letter, and if Jackson received no order, he would not act. Finally, association with this religious fanatic made most people uncomfortable. He seemed to be almost too good, in a religious sense, for the community.

A few years later events took place that must have thrust the citizens of Lexington into a state of shock. Their peculiar professor earned the title of General Stonewall Jackson and fought his famous Valley Campaign, which stands as one of the most brilliant military maneuvers in the history of the profession of arms. In three short months General Jackson marched his "foot cavalry" [12] 600 miles, defeated four Union armies, and captured 4,000 prisoners and 10,000 arms, throwing the Union strategy into a state of confusion.[13] With

3

Jackson's small army of about 3,000 men he diverted a Northern force of more than 25,000 troops from an almost fatal attack on Richmond.[14] The people in Lexington must have wondered how this religious fanatic could become one of the South's greatest generals.

NOTES

1. G.R.F. Henderson, *Stonewall Jackson and the American Civil War, Vol. 1* (New York: Longmans, Green and Company, 1919), pp. 68–69.
2. John Esten Cooke, *Stonewall Jackson: A Military Biography* (New York: D. Appleton and Company, 1876), p. 23.
3. Ibid. p. 28.
4. Ibid.
5. Ibid.
6. Paul Miller Offill, "Stonewall Jackson: A Case Study in Religious Motivation and Its Effect on Confederate Leadership and Morale." (M.S. Thesis, University of Pittsburgh, 1961), p. 5.
7. Ibid.
8. Cooke, p. 28.
9. Ibid.
10. Offill, p. 49.
11. Lenior Chambers, *Stonewall Jackson*, Vol. 1 (New York: W. Morrow, 1959), p. 236.
12. Cooke, p. 274.
13. Ibid. pp. 193–196.
14. Ibid.

CHAPTER TWO

Boyhood, 1824–1842

I shall not go back anymore.
Thomas J. Jackson

ORPHAN

Thomas Jonathan Jackson was born on January 21, 1824, in Clarksburg, Virginia. No records were kept about his birth, but this was the date that he felt was probably correct. [1] Thomas's father, Jonathan, was a lawyer in the young, growing community. Jonathan, a poor manager of money, had financial difficulty in the later years of his life. [2]

When Thomas was very young, perhaps only two or three years old, his father died and left a widow, Julia Neal Jackson, with three children and almost no money.[3] The family lived on charity that was given to them by relatives and friends. Young Thomas heard much discussion about the poor Jackson family and conjecture of what would become of them. It was during this time that he began to develop his strong ambition. Thomas resolved that he would change the reputation of the Jackson family line, and it was a commitment that he never forgot.[4] Mrs. Julia N. Jackson married Captain Blake B. Woodson in 1830. Her new husband was a lawyer and popular socially; but he had no money.[5] Because of this lack of means, the new Mrs. Woodson sent her children to live with relatives. Thomas, who was then six years old, spent time with a number of different families.[6] A year later Thomas's mother died, leaving the young child a penniless orphan. [7]

After the death of their mother, Thomas and his sister, Laura, went to live at the residence of their stepgrandmother. [8] The home was located in Lewis County and was managed by Thomas's uncle, Cummins Jackson. Uncle Cummins was kind to the young orphans, and eventually Thomas' brother, Warren, came to live there also. [9]

The uncle noticed a profound determination beginning to develop within Thomas. The loss of his father and mother as well as the separation of the family were terrible blows for a young child. But Thomas was learning to stand up in the storm, and he dedicated his life to becoming the man that his father never was. Cummins Jackson caught the vision of this dream and helped Thomas as much as he could. [10]

EARLY DETERMINATION

It is interesting to analyze the character of Jackson at this early age because even at this time traits began to appear that would remain indelibly attached to him throughout his life. Thomas moved quite often in his childhood, and some of the homes where he lived were much more pleasant than others. A statement that he often made in connection with his unpleasant relatives was, "I shall not go back anymore." [11] The determination that seemed evident in many of the members of the Jackson family was inherited by Thomas.

The society of Lewis County during the 1820s and 1830s had the typical frontier atmosphere. There were many horse races and country dances in addition to the farm work. Thomas took part in these agrarian activities but seemed to remain

6

separated to a large extent from the lax attitudes that accompanied them.[12] A deep religious feeling was developing within Jackson, even at this early age. Theology allowed him to overcome much of the insecurity and inferiority that were thrust upon him as a victim of cruel circumstance. Jackson's minister, as a spiritual guide, replaced his lost parents; and his inferiority complex was overcome to a large extent by gaining and expounding on a thorough knowledge of the Bible. The biblical wisdom and quotations that he could share with others gave him a sense of worth and self-respect.[13]

Cummins Jackson provided Thomas with the opportunity to attend the local school, and the young man took advantage of it. His father had been a student of law and his mother was a student of the scriptures, so Thomas felt at home in the classroom. He worked arduously and seemed to be the complete opposite of his brother, Warren, who was an extremely restless boy.[14] The motive behind Jackson's studiousness was a desire for self-improvement. He was obsessed with the idea that he must make something of himself.[15]

Jackson's friends in the small community recalled some of the traits that were prominent in his character. Most of his actions were considered good, and he was looked up to as an example. Thomas was a born leader and his charismatic personality was noticed. He had the courage to stand for a principle that he thought was right and, again, this alluded to his determination. Jackson was not brilliant, and it took him a long time to learn in the classroom; but once he grasped a concept it was permanently impressed on his memory. Thomas took plenty of time making decisions, but once they were made he acted quickly toward the accomplishment of his goal.[16]

So this was the young, determined Tom Jackson. A boy working to earn self-respect which had been lost in poor circumstances.[17] This key to Jackson's character foreshadowed much of his later life and was the motivation behind many of his actions.

CONSTABLE

Thomas enjoyed living with his uncle Cummins on the Jackson farm. The work kept him active, and he developed a strong body. During this time he became rather independent for a young man. It was probably a result of the great trust that Thomas's uncle had in him and the way that Cummins relied on him. Tom did much of the farm work without direct supervision from his uncle, and this was an asset.[18]

The independent personality of Jackson continued to develop, and he began to look for a means to support himself. This did not result from a conflict with his uncle. He had a high degree of respect and admiration for Cummins Jackson, but Thomas wanted to make his own way. With the help of friends and relatives, he obtained the position of constable in Lewis County. [19]

Seventeen is not a ripe old age to assume the role of a minor sheriff, but Jackson managed the responsibility quite well. His duties included serving warrants, collecting debts, and summoning witnesses. Thomas enjoyed riding his horse throughout the county and hoped that this would help to restore his health. A few years earlier he had begun to suffer from chronic dyspepsia, which continued throughout his life.[20]

Thomas noticed that his work as a constable was more beneficial to his health than to his character. He was away from the atmosphere of his home during much of the time and, of course, he was forced to associate with the worst people in the community. Tom recognized that the poor character traits of the citizens with whom he worked were becoming

8

his own, and this fact concerned him greatly. [21]

Because the work as constable was so abhorrent to Jackson, he began to look for other possibilities.[22] Thomas always had a desire to continue his education and, coincidentally, a vacancy developed at the United States Military Academy. A boy from Jackson's district quit at West Point, and someone was needed to fill the place. Cummins Jackson was a good friend of their congressman, Samuel S. Hays, and this helped Thomas to obtain a letter of recommendation from him in 1842. [23]

DESIRE FOR EDUCATION

Young Thomas realized that securing an education was the gateway to a profession, and now there was a possibility that he would have this opportunity. He left the Jackson farm and traveled to Washington, D.C., for the purpose of meeting with Congressman Hays. The representative introduced Thomas to the secretary of war, John C. Spencer, who naturally had great influence at the Military Academy. During their conversation Mr. Hays referred to Jackson's lack of education but also stressed the young man's determination.[24] The secretary of war said to Thomas, "Sir, you have a good name. Go to West Point, and the first man who insults you, knock him down, and have it charged to my account."[25]

Congressman Hays was very hospitable toward Jackson and asked him to spend some time with the representative, so that he could see Washington, D.C. Naturally, Thomas appreciated this offer, but all that he had on his mind was realizing his desire to obtain an education. Jackson told Mr. Hays that a view from the top of the Capitol Building would be sufficient at this time. After a short look over the city, Thomas was on his way to the Point of the Hudson. [26]

9

Jackson arrived at West Point dressed in crude farm clothes and carrying a letter of introduction to the faculty from Mr. Hays. The letter attested to Thomas's fine character and recommended that allowances be made for his poor educational background. The officers at the Military Academy were impressed with the letter from the congressman and gave an exceptionally lenient examination to Jackson. After the examination Thomas was admitted, and his impossible dream was swiftly becoming a reality. [27]

Notes

1. Mary Anna Jackson, *Memoirs of Stonewall Jackson* (Louisville: The Prentice Press, 1895), p. 14.
2. Cooke, p. 10.
3. Thomas Jackson Arnold, *Early Life and Letters of General Thomas J. Jackson* (Richmond: Fleming H. Revell Company, 1916), p. 14.
4. Offill, p. 3.
5. Jackson, p. 15.
6. Ibid. p. 16.
7. Henderson, pp. 16–17.
8. Jackson, p. 19.
9. Ibid. p. 20.
10. Offill, p. 24.
11. Arnold, p. 30.
12. Ibid. p. 47.
13. Offill, p. 31.
14. Jackson, p. 22.
15. Ibid. p. 24.
16. Henry Kyd Douglas, *I Rode With Stonewall* (Chapel Hill: The University of North Carolina Press, 1940), p. 10.
17. J. William Jones, *Christ in the Camp* (Atlanta: The Martin and Hoyt Company, 1887), p. 11.
18. Jackson, p. 26.
19. Ibid. pp. 27–28.
20. Henderson, p. 11.
21. R.L. Dabney, *Life and Campaigns of Lieut.-Gen. Thomas J. Jackson* (New York: Blelock and Company, 1866), p. 23.

22. Jackson, p. 29.
23. Arnold, p. 52.
24. Jackson, p. 32.
25. Henderson, p. 13.
26. Jackson, p. 32.
27. Ibid.

CHAPTER THREE

United States Military Academy, 1842–1846

You may be whatever you resolve to be.
Thomas J. Jackson

JACKSON'S CHARACTER

Thomas realized, even before he reached West Point, that he would be looked upon as a country hayseed.[1] But his homespun appearance hid the character of a man who had not come to quit. The corps of cadets found Jackson ready for the intensive mental and physical harassment. It was not long before the tricks performed by the upperclassmen ended. [2]

Many insights into the personality of Jackson come to light by examining his cadetship. Thomas's associates remembered him as an exceptionally reserved person. With one or two people Jackson would talk freely, and he enjoyed debating within a small group. But when Jackson was around a large number of people, he was a silent observer.[3] Usually Jackson did not seem aggressive, but most of his friends noticed how inflexible his character was. If Thomas felt he was correct in principle, no amount of persuasion could change his opinion.[4]

Jackson also developed great powers of concentration at the Academy. One of his former roommates stated:

> No one I have ever known . . . could so perfectly withdraw his mind from surrounding objects or influences, and so thoroughly involve his whole being in the subject under consideration. [5]

Jackson was conscientious in almost everything that he did. Of course his rifle was always kept immaculate and ready for inspection. One day a cadet replaced Jackson's weapon with a dirty old rifle. The dishonest cadet did not know that Thomas had placed a special mark on his weapon to identify it. At the next inspection of arms, Jackson's rifle was found and the cadet lied in an attempt to cover up his action. This made Jackson furious and he demanded that the cadet be court-martialled in order to expel him. Finally, after hours of persuasion by both cadets and officers, Thomas changed his mind. This was one of the few times that Jackson's temper exploded during his cadetship, but one can see that it was capable of running a very destructive course.[6]

When Thomas was an upperclassman, his roommate became a cadet orderly-sergeant for their company. One of the cadet sergeant's duties was to take the roll call at meal formations, and the roommate told Jackson that he would not have to attend reveille from then on. Most cadets would look with great anticipation at this opportunity to sleep late each morning, but Thomas never used the privilege. His sense of honor would not allow him to accept the easier way. [7]

Jackson seemed to associate well with most of the people at the Military Academy. A former classmate of his said that Thomas never had "a hard word or bad feeling from a cadet or professor."[8] Of course this is not completely true, but it does demonstrate how the cadets felt about Jackson. "Old Jack,"[9] as they called him, was a person who could win respect and confidence easily. He was also an earnest and straightforward person. These traits, combined with his ability to place honor above self, won for him the admiration of many people. [10]

The picture of Jackson painted to this point portrays him as a near-perfect person; naturally he was not. Thomas's graduation party in a Washington, D.C., hotel was a wild affair. He and his friends were drinking when one of his other classmates dropped by the room for a visit. The visitor was surprised to find one of the celebrators passed out on a bed. "Old Jack" [11] and a friend, clothed only in their underwear, were singing "Benny Hans, Oh" ("Benny Havens, Oh") [12] and dancing a "barefoot backstep" [13] to the tune. This is the only recorded experience of Jackson taking part in a drunken brawl, and it is probably with the memory of this experience that he stated to a staff member later during the Civil War that he feared liquor much more than enemy bullets. [14]

DYSPEPSIA

Jackson was plagued with poor health throughout most of his relatively short life. This was undoubtedly one of the reasons that he was so peculiar in his actions. The humbling effect of his weak body was also possibly a catalyst in his search for religious truth. Many of Jackson's illnesses will be written about in this book, but the one that was a chronic problem for him during much of his life was dyspepsia.

This abdominal disease appeared while Thomas lived on the old Jackson farm, and it continued through his cadetship at West Point. In fact, the intensive mental and physical harassment at the Academy made his health much worse. It was because of this that Jackson formed and followed strict health rules. [15] He was extremely careful with his choice of food, and his daily schedule usually involved some type of strenuous exercise. Many afternoons, Thomas was seen by his peers walking briskly over the hills at the Point of the Hudson. The exercise was good for his muscles; but, more importantly, it served to tranquilize his nervous condition.[16]

Jackson's attempt to control his dyspepsia made him appear eccentric to many people. Some of his study habits seemed rather odd. Thomas would never lean over his books because he felt this might disturb his sensitive stomach. His roommates thought it was ironic to see this meticulously conscientious cadet slouch in their room while he studied; but, after considering Jackson's stomach condition, the posture was quite reasonable. At the mess hall Thomas would often eat a large amount of one or two items on the menu and leave the rest of the food for his friends. Naturally they felt that this eating habit was peculiar; however, it was another attempt by Jackson to pacify his nervous stomach.[17]

Thomas did not tell the cadets much about his chronic health problem; perhaps it embarrassed him. A simple explanation might have prevented much of the gossip that spread in the corps as a result of his unusual actions. However, Thomas wrote about his stomach in many letters to his sister, Laura. In one message these words are recorded:

My disease is improving, for which I feel thankful to *Omnipotent God,* from whom every blessing cometh. I believe that my infirmity is dyspepsia, not of a dangerous character, but of a nervous one. . . . [18]

The disease that Jackson wrote about continued to bother him throughout his life.

WORK

Despite the peculiar actions of Thomas because of his chronic illness, he got along well with most of the cadets. In fact, he found getting along socially much easier than adapting to the academic requirements of the faculty. Jackson's educational background was poor, and this made it hard for him to compete. He began his cadetship with "The Immortals,"[19] the lowest section in his class, and it was only because of exceptionally hard work that he was able to maintain a place in that section.[20] Jackson later stated that he "studied very hard for what he got at West Point."[21] With a great number of cadets failing each year, Thomas did not expect to last long. He thought about going back to Lewis County as a failure, and this concerned him greatly. Thomas even prepared what he would say to his friends. As Mary Anna Jackson notes, "If they had been there, and found it as hard as he did, they would have failed too."[22] Finally, Thomas stopped worrying and started to work; he did not fail.

Jackson progressed academically every year, and his military record was not poor either. During his entire cadetship at West Point, he received 48 demerits, which is quite a favorable record. In Thomas's fourth class (freshman) year, he was fifty-first in a class of eighty-three members, academically. By the end of his third class year, Jackson was standing thirtieth in a class of seventy-eight. He rose to a ranking of twenty out of sixty-five cadets in his second class year. Finally, Jackson graduated seventeen in a class of sixty men. Some of his friends speculated that if there had been one more year, Thomas would have been first in his class. [23]

Jackson worked hard for his academic progress at the Point, and he was proud of his record. He did not talk much about it with his friends because he was naturally a quiet person. But each time progress was realized, Thomas would send a letter to his sister and give her the complete details. [24] Behind this humble, unaggressive exterior that Thomas displayed to his friends there was an egotistical, determined young man. He would work to almost any length to accomplish his goals.

ETHICAL CODE

Thomas had an affinity for self-improvement in almost every aspect of his life. During his cadetship he compiled a book containing rules and maxims of an ethical nature; he hoped to use these to elevate his character. Most of the book is about personal appearance, choosing associates, and actions in public. Jackson's most well known maxim is, "You can be whatever you resolve to be."[25] The contents of the entire book offer deep insight into the attitudes and ideas that he had at this time.

The cadet wrote some interesting rules in one section of his book:

> Through life let your principal object be the discharge of duty.—Disregard public opinion when it interferes with your duty.—Endeavor to be at peace with all men.—Sacrifice your life rather than your word.—Endeavor to do well everything which you undertake.—Never speak disrespectfully of any one without a cause.—Spare no effort to suppress selfishness, unless that effort would entail sorrow.—Let your conduct towards men have some uniformity.—Temperance: Eat not to dullness, drink not to elevation.—Silence: Speak but what may benefit others or yourself; avoid trifling conversation.—Resolve to perform what you ought; perform without fail what you resolve.—Frugality: make no expense but to do good to others or yourself; waste nothing.—Industry: Lose no time; be always employed in something useful; cut off unnecessary actions.—Sincerity: Use no hurtful deceit; think innocently and justly, and if you speak, speak accordingly.—Justice: Wrong no man by doing injuries, or omitting the benefits that are your duty.—Moderation: avoid extremes; forbear resenting injuries as much as you think they deserve.—Cleanliness: Tolerate no uncleanliness in body, clothes or habitation.—Tranquility: Be not disturbed at trifles, not at accidents, common or unavoidable.[26]

Jackson recorded some "motives to action,"[27] which offer further insight about him:

> . . . 1. Regard to your own happiness. 2. Regard to the family to which you belong. 3. Strive to attain a very great elevation of character. 4. Fix upon a high standard of action and character.[28]

Some additional rules were associated with this theme:

> It is man's highest interest not to violate, or attempt to violate, the rules which Infinite wisdom has laid down. The means by which men are to attain great elevation may be classed in three divisions—physical, mental, moral. Whatever relates to the improvement of the mind, belongs to the second. The formation of good manners and virtuous habits constitutes the third.[29]

Thomas wrote about making choices concerning friends:

> . . . 1. A man is known by the company he keeps. 2. Be cautious in your selection. 3. There is danger of catching the habits of your associates.
>
> 4. Seek those who are intelligent and virtuous; and, if possible, those who are a little above you, especially in moral excellence.
>
> 5. It is not desirable to have a large number of intimate friends; you may have many acquaintances, but few intimate friends. If you have *one* who is what he should be, you are comparatively happy.
>
> That friendship may be at once fond and lasting, there must not only be virtue in each, but virtue of the same kind: not only the same end must be proposed, but the same means must be approached. [30]

Not all of the cadet's rules and maxims were original. Some were copied from a book about etiquette titled *Politeness and Good-breeding:*

Good-breeding, or true politeness, is the art of showing men by external signs the internal regard we have for them. It arises from good sense, improved by good company. It must be acquired by practice and not by books.

Be kind, condescending, and affable. Any one who has anything to say to a fellow-being, to say it with kind feeling and sincere desire to please; and this, whenever it is done, will atone for much awkwardness in the manner of expression.

Good-breeding is opposed to selfishness, vanity or pride. Never weary your company by talking too long or too frequently. Always look people in the face when addressing them, and generally when they address you. Never engross the whole conversation to yourself. Say as little of yourself and friends as possible.

Make it a rule never to accuse without due consideration any body [sic] or association of men. Never try to appear more wise or learned than the rest of the company, not that you should affect ignorance, but endeavor to remain within your own proper sphere.[31]

Anyone who has read a biography about Jackson will recognize the penetrating depth of insight contained in the preceding paragraphs. The lines allude to many of his character traits: quietness, conscientiousness, industry, sincerity, and others. It is also evident from the man's actions and letters that his rules and maxims had a direct effect on his life. Thomas once wrote to his sister about the importance of not becoming depressed:

Be not discouraged by disappointments and difficulties, but on the contrary let each stimulate you to greater exertions for attaining noble ends, and an approving conscience at least will be your reward.[32]

NOTES

1. Allen Tate, *Stonewall Jackson* (New York: G.P. Putnam's Sons, 1956), pp. 29–30.
2. Henderson, p. 14.
3. Dabney, p. 35.
4. Ibid. p. 38.
5. Henderson, p. 20.
6. Ibid. p. 19.
7. Ibid.
8. Henderson, p. 20.
9. Ibid.
10. Ibid.
11. Chambers, p. 76.
12. Ibid.
13. Ibid.
14. Henderson, p. 60.
15. Ibid. p. 21.
16. Dabney, p. 36.
17. Henderson, p. 21.
18. Arnold, p. 157.
19. Henderson, p. 15.
20. Ibid.
21. Jackson, pp. 33–34.
22. Ibid.
23. West Point Library, Class Standings and Records of Thomas Jonathan Jackson, 1842–1846 (West Point: United States Military Academy).
24. Jackson to sister, Laura, August 2, 1845. Thomas Jonathan Jackson, Personal Letters, Military Correspondence and Reports. Special Collections, Preston Library, Virginia Military Institute, Lexington, Virginia. Hereafter referred to as Jackson Collection.
25. Henderson, p. 21.
26. Jackson, pp. 35–37.
27. Ibid.
28. Ibid.
29. Ibid.
30. Ibid.
31. Jackson, pp. 37–38.
32. Jackson to sister, Laura, September 8, 1844, Jackson Collection.

CHAPTER FOUR

United States Army, 1846–1851

Duty is ours, consequences are God's.
Thomas J. Jackson

PROMOTION

During Jackson's first year at the Military Academy he began to think more about the future. Thomas was not particularly interested in an army career; the main reason that he came to West Point was to become educated. Jackson wanted to practice law or enter business, but since he had no capital, he decided to remain in the army for a few years.[1]

A short time after Jackson was commissioned a second lieutenant in 1846 the Mexican War began, and he was ordered to report with Company K, First Artillery Regiment. This army unit traveled through Pennsylvania, down the Mississippi and Ohio rivers to Louisiana, and then to Texas prior to embarking for Mexico. The regiment reached Mexico quite rapidly, and the young officer was soon putting the theories in his West Point textbooks to practice.[2]

Captain John B. Magruder captured a Mexican field battery, and command of this battery was given to the captain by General Winfield Scott for the young man's gallantry. There was a vacancy for a second lieutenant in this battery. Most officers did not like to serve with the brave captain because he was quick to anger and nearly worked his staff to death. However, once Jackson learned of the new position, he applied for it and was immediately transferred.[3] Years later when Jackson was asked why he wanted to serve under Magruder he replied:

> I wanted to see active service, to be near the enemy in the fight; and when I heard that John Magruder had got his battery I bent all my energies to be with him, for I knew if any fighting was to be done, Magruder would be "on hand."[4]

The lieutenant did not have a great love for the profession of arms, but if he had to fight, he wanted to get in the thick of it and help end the conflict quickly.

Jackson's service under Magruder was one continuously distinguished tour of duty. With reference to an early engagement with the enemy, Captain Magruder wrote:

> Lieutenant Jackson, commanding the second section of the battery, who had opened fire upon the enemy's works from a position on the right, hearing our fire still further in front, advanced in handsome style, and kept up the fire with equal briskness and effect. His conduct was equally conspicuous during the whole day, and I cannot too highly commend him to the Major-General's [sic] favourable consideration.[5]

A different officer wrote about Jackson's conduct in the same engagement:

> The advanced section of the battery, under command of the brave Lieutenant Jackson, was dreadfully cut up, and almost

disabled . . . Captain Magruder's battery, one section of which was served with great gallantry by himself and the other by his brave lieutenant [*sic*], Jackson, in face of a galling fire from the enemy's position, did invaluable service.[6]

As one can observe from the reports about the lieutenant, he displayed an exceptional degree of courage. Many times he would walk up and down the line of his section shouting, "There is no danger: See! I am not hit."[7] Jackson was promoted to first lieutenant "for gallant and meritorious conduct in the siege of Vera Cruz."[8] Later his section fought in another battle near Chapultepec, which lasted for two days. During this conflict the young lieutenant commanded his men with such great skill that he was subsequently promoted to the brevet rank of captain.[9] After the fighting at Chapultepec, Magruder wrote these lines about Jackson:

I beg leave to call the attention of the Major-General commanding the division to the conduct of Lieutenant Jackson of the First Artillery. If devotion, industry, talent and gallantry are the highest qualities of a soldier, then is he entitled to the distinction which their possession confers. I have been ably seconded in all operations of the battery by him; and upon this occasion, when circumstances placed him in command for a short time of an independent section, he proved himself eminently worthy of it.[10]

For this performance Jackson won the brevet rank of major. During these months, the young West Pointer was promoted more frequently than any officer of the United States Army in Mexico.[11]

At one time during the war, Jackson was ordered to remain behind and garrison the town of Jalapa. This was extremely distasteful to him, and he wrote to his sister:

I throw myself into the hands of an all wise God and hope that it may yet be for the better. It may have been one of His means of diminishing my excessive ambition; and after having accomplished His purpose, whatever it may be, He then in His infinite wisdom may gratify my heart.[12]

One can see from these lines that the major had developed a deep sense of trust in his Father in Heaven. However, he was not a perfect Christian soldier. A short time later Jackson was asked if he ever had reservations about killing women and children with his artillery. The officer replied sharply: "None whatsoever. What business have I with what happens to noncombatants. My duty is to obey orders."[13] This seems to be a rather cold response from a Christian man. Jackson was also one of the most egotistical soldiers in Mexico, and this came to light years later in a conversation. He was asked if he experienced fear in battle when so many were falling around him. His reply was:

No, the only anxiety of which I was conscious during the engagement was a fear least I should not meet danger enough to make my conduct conspicuous.[14]

MEXICO CITY

The war had finally ended, and many of the United States troops were stationed in Mexico City until the terms of the agreement between the two nations were negotiated. Jackson had distinguished himself in the heat of battle; now he was ready for some rest and relaxation. The young West Pointer seemed to enjoy his tour of duty at the foreign capital.[15]

The adjustment from war to peace was not an easy transition for the troops to make. Naturally it took time for them to replace their hatred for the enemy with a feeling of friendship. The Mexican people were much more dynamic in this respect than the American soldiers. After a few weeks the two former enemies began to associate quite well together. Even the quiet young Jackson met with the Mexican people and learned about their way of life.[16]

The major found the Mexican life-style of the 1840s to be intriguing. He had extremely large feet which made him clumsy, but he still learned many of the Mexican dances. There was some question in Jackson's mind about whether it was right for a Christian to dance, but he disregarded this doubt temporarily. The young officer was also interested in the Spanish language of the Mexican nation. He spent a large amount of his free time learning the language and reached a high degree of proficiency with it. Throughout the rest of his life many of his letters were spiced with Spanish words.[17]

Jackson was a restless person, and even in the quiet, slow atmosphere of Mexico he kept busy. His desire for self-improvement was never satisfied, and this provided the motivation for his activity. In addition to acquainting himself with the customs and language of the Mexican people, the officer also studied their Catholic religion. This was an important stage in the life of Jackson because it formally initiated his religious awakening.[18]

RELIGIOUS AWAKENING

Colonel Frank Taylor, commander of the First Artillery, was the initial person to formally guide Jackson in a spiritual manner.[19] The colonel acted in a fatherly manner toward his staff. The young officers had many opportunities to hear his theological beliefs and fervent prayers. Jackson was a rather insecure man, having lost both of his parents in early childhood, so the actions of Taylor were well-suited to his needs. With the colonel acting as the catalyst, the major's religious awakening began.[20]

Jackson had no significant prejudice for any sect of Christianity. Therefore, he decided to conduct a detailed investigation of each denomination before choosing one.[21] This independent attitude would probably have shocked Jackson's Presbyterian ancestors, but he payed little attention to the opinions of men when he felt that he was correct in principle.

The Catholic Church was dominant in Mexico, and so this was where the major's religious search began. He soon developed a pleasant friendship with many of the priests in the local church and they even invited him to live at their chapel temporarily. After discussing Catholicism extensively with the priests, Jackson had several interviews with the Archbishop of Mexico. The young officer was impressed with the sincerity and knowledge of the Catholic clergy, but he could not accept their doctrine of Christianity. So Jackson left Mexico without professing a belief in any Christian sect.[22]

Major Jackson's next tour of duty was at Fort Hamilton, New York; and, here again, Colonel Frank Taylor was his commanding officer. Therefore, Jackson's search for truth in Christianity was eagerly continued. It is doubtful that the young officer's sole motive was to please his devout commander. Jackson had developed a sincere interest in theology.

There was some question in the major's mind about whether he had been baptized in his early childhood. After reading in the Bible about the importance of baptism, he wanted to be certain that this ordinance had been performed.[23] However, of equal importance to Jackson was the fact that he did not want to become a member of any religious sect at that time. He still was not satisfied with any of the denominations that he had studied. The major talked with an Episcopal minister about his religious dilemma, and the reverend assured him that he would baptize Jackson a Christian without Jackson incurring any obligation to the Episcopal Church.[24] In the baptismal records of the Episcopal Church near Fort Hamilton, these lines are written:

> On Sunday, 29th day of April, 1849, I baptized Thomas Jefferson [sic] Jackson, Major in the U.S. Army. Sponsors, Colonels Dimick and Taylor.[25]

The record was signed by "Mr. Schofield."[26] Obviously Jackson's middle name was recorded in error; it was Jonathan rather than Jefferson.

Some significant facts are learned about Jackson from this period of time, which is considered to be his religious awakening. The awakening was more an initiation of his search for a true sect than it was his gaining a belief in Christianity. Even though the major came from an unreligious environment, he always had a firm belief in God.[27] Another important point that comes to light is the fact that Jackson was an independent person and he did not simply adopt the Presbyterian Church of his ancestors. He actually studied the Catholic Church first.[28] Finally, and perhaps most importantly, the officer would not accept a denomination until he was certain from his exhaustive study that it was true. He felt that he had been baptized a Christian, not an Episcopalian, by the cooperative minister.[29]

POOR HEALTH

The Virginia Military Institute was in need of a professor for the chair of natural philosophy (physics) in 1851. Once the vacancy became known, it was greatly sought after. Applicants for the position included George B. McClellan, Jesse L. Reno and W.S. Rosecrans.[30] At this same time Thomas Jackson was

27

experiencing poor health in the army, and this was probably the main reason that caused him to announce his candidacy for the chair.[31] He still had a chronic dyspepsia condition, but the officer's main problem was his eyes. They became extremely weak, and he was also bothered with unusual spots that impaired his vision. Because of this problem with his eyes, Jackson had to take great caution in using them. He would never read at night, and during the day, even though there was plenty of light, he exercised discretion. This condition had a profoundly negative effect on his ability to conduct his duties as an officer in the army.[32]

Jackson's problem with his vision stemmed back to his cadetship at West Point. He read extensively at the Academy, and this placed a great burden on his eyes. After his graduation he retained a desire to study, and this eventually resulted in a severe problem with his vision.

Once the major had made up his mind to apply for the professorship at the Virginia Military Institute, he worked unceasingly to gain acceptance. Every friend who might have an influence on the decision of the board of visitors was contacted and encouraged to inform the board of their support for Jackson.[33] The young officer may not have been as well qualified for the position as some of the other applicants, but his attempt to fill the vacancy was as untiring as his conduct in the Mexican War. The board of visitors of the Virginia Military Institute, in March of 1851, announced that Thomas Jonathan Jackson would fill the vacancy of professor of artillery tactics and natural philosophy.[34] Naturally, Jackson was extremely happy because this meant that even with his poor health he could continue to serve in a semimilitary environment. His earlier reservations about remaining in the military had all vanished.

NOTES

1. Offill, p. 35.
2. Arnold, p. 79.
3. Ibid. p. 93.
4. Henderson, p. 39.
5. Ibid.
6. Jackson, p. 42.
7. Henderson, p. 41.
8. Ibid. p. 29.
9. Arnold, p. 103.
10. Ibid. p. 113.
11. Dabney, p. 51.
12. Jackson to sister, Laura, May 25, 1847, Jackson Collection.
13. Chambers, Vol. 1, p. 116.
14. Henderson, p. 46.
15. Ibid. p. 50.
16. Jackson to sister, Laura, March 23, 1848, Jackson Collection.
17. Henderson, p. 52.
18. Ibid. p. 53.
19. Jackson to uncle, September, 1846, Jackson Collection.
20. Henderson, pp. 52–53.
21. Ibid. p. 53.
22. Ibid.
23. Ibid p. 55.
24. Ibid.
25. Jackson, p. 49.
26. Ibid.
27. Offill, p. 26.
28. Henderson, p. 53.
29. Ibid. p. 55.
30. Arnold, p. 173.
31. Cooke, p. 19.
32. Jackson, p. 56
33. Arnold, p. 74.
34. Henderson, p. 55.

CHAPTER FIVE

Lexington, 1851–1861

> *I would go without my hat.*
> Thomas J. Jackson

VIRGINIA MILITARY INSTITUTE

After Major Thomas J. Jackson was discharged from the United States Army, he traveled to Lexington, Virginia. Although he was officially no longer in the army, Jackson still thought about a future career in the profession of arms. While talking with some friends, he stated that an officer with a good reputation who entered a semimilitary profession in peacetime would be better prepared for war than one who stayed in the "treadmill" atmosphere of an army post.[1] At the Virginia Military Institute the major taught gunnery as well as the sciences, and he found this beneficial for his military preparation.[2]

Jackson had never taught a class before he came to the Institute. The courses assigned to him were rigorous by nature, and some of his peers wondered if he was hesitant about the enormous task before him. In reply to their question the major remarked, "No, I expect to be able to study sufficiently in advance of my class; for one can always do what he wills to accomplish."[3] This is the kind of attitude that Jackson had in everything that he attempted.

The young professor's confidence did not make him a good instructor, however. He was a quiet, serious person and it was difficult for him to adjust to the role of a teacher.[4] Jackson's explanations were always brief, and if a cadet did not understand, the major would simply repeat his former, short response. This repetitive method of teaching was not conducive to an atmosphere of learning. The professor knew that on the battlefield short, precise orders are priceless, but he did not realize that in the classroom this type of communication creates difficulty.[5]

Jackson's personality was just as odd as his method of teaching. He always sat straight in his chair and never seemed to move. When a question was asked, the professor became almost overly attentive until the question was ended. Then, he would meditate for a few minutes to form an answer. His courses were difficult and required about six books, but Jackson never referred to a text during class. In his answers to questions he would recite exactly the relevant lines from the books.[6]

One day something unusual happened. The cadets managed to get the major off the subject by bringing up the Mexican War. A cadet asked, "That was a very hot place, wasn't it, Major?" Jackson replied, "Yes, very hot." Another cadet inquired, "Why didn't you run, Major?" With that question the class began to laugh. The professor answered:

I was not ordered to do so. If I had been ordered to run, I would have done so; but I was directed to hold my position, and I had no right to abandon it.[7]

Of course the young cadets did not comprehend the major's deep sense of duty.

Other instructional techniques of the professor were remembered by his students. Jackson's experiments were not interesting and often ended in complete failure. When they did not work, he would laugh as loudly as the rest of the class.[8] The major's examinations were much better than his experiments. The students recalled that Jackson's questions were carefully chosen and usually fair. The tests never contained extraneous lines and reminded the cadets of his brief explanations.[9]

Jackson was definitely not a good instructor, according to the superindent, Colonel Francis H. Smith. The superintendent wrote:

> As a professor of Natural and Experimental Philosophy, Major Jackson was not a success. He had not the qualifications needed for so important a chair. He was no teacher, and he lacked the tact required to get along with his classes. Every officer and every cadet respected him, however, for his many sterling qualities. He was a brave man, a conscientious man, and a good man, but he was no professor. . . . [10]

A cadet also wrote about Jackson's odd, but basically good nature:

Hick, alias Hickory, alias Old Jack,
Alias, Major T. J. Jackson

Like some rough brute that ranged the forest wild
So rude and uncouth, so purely Nature's child
Is Hickory, and yet methinks I see
The stamp of genius on his brow, and he
With his wild glance and keen but quiet eye
Draws forth from secret sources, where they lie
These thoughts and feelings of the human heart
Most virtuous, good and free from guilty art

There's something in his very mode of life
So accurate, steady, void of care and strife
That fills my heart with love for him
Who bears his honors meekly. . . . [11]

So this was the odd, incompetent professor at the Virginia
Military Institute during the 1850s.

HOME LIFE

Jackson's home life was, in many respects, as unique as his
teaching career. The professor felt that his house should be a
house of order, so everything was conducted in a systematic
manner. Each morning he would rise at six o'clock and immediately offer a personal prayer. Following this prayer,
Jackson would have a cold bath, no matter what the weather
was. Next, the peculiar professor would go for a brisk walk;
and, again, he conducted his exercise with no regard to the
weather. Promptly at seven o'clock a prayer was scheduled
for all servants and family members. If anyone was late for
this religious gathering, it was conducted without them. After
family prayer, breakfast was held, and then Jackson would
walk to the Institute. His classes lasted from eight to eleven
o'clock; and after they were over, he would immediately return
home. When he arrived at his house, the professor would
begin a period of study that lasted until one o'clock. This
academic work included a reading exercise in the Bible and
a review of his textbooks. Jackson's wife commented that there
were many pencil marks in his Bible and textbooks, so it is
apparent that the major labored diligently over the materials.
During this time he refused to be interrupted, and he stood
concentrating in front of a high desk. Following the study
period, Jackson and his family would have lunch. For a half

hour after this meal he would indulge in conversation. Then, Jackson would inspect the family garden behind his house or his farm, located near Lexington. The professor would often engage in the agricultural work along with his slaves. When he returned home, the family would have their dinner and then another short period of conversation. Jackson felt that it was bad for his health to work right after he ate. This theory probably related directly to his chronic dyspepsia condition. He would begin to study when the short relaxation time was over. However, during this study session the professor never used a book. He simply went over, in his mind, the study that he had conducted earlier in the day. The major did this because his eyes were still weak, and he was afraid that he might become completely blind if they were used excessively. The mental study was beneficial; the professor increased his power of concentration and memorization greatly. After this academic work, Jackson would retire to bed at an early hour. The most unique aspect of this schedule of activities was its constant and exact repetition. People in Lexington could set their watches as the major walked by their homes on his way to the Institute.[12]

The manner in which Jackson conducted himself around his home is interesting. He was strict and demanding with his slaves.[13] If one of them left a room without closing the door, the master would let him walk completely through the house and then call him back to close it. Naturally, he found that the servants learned quickly from this method.[14] Jackson's wife, the former Mary Anna Morrison, was surprised with the change in her husband at home. She once wrote that "his buoyancy and sportiveness were quite a revelation to me when I beame a sharer in the privacy of his innermost life."[15] Many times Jackson would hide behind a door, and as she walked nearby, he would jump out and throw his arms around her.[16] The peculiar professor probably needed this emotional release from his strict schedule.

34

Jackson was a kind, understanding father with his family. The stern professor and strict slave owner would soften in their presence, and his wife stated that his strongest chastisement was, "Ah! That is not the way to be happy."[17] One can observe from the preceding accounts that Jackson developed a dynamic personality during his decade in Lexington.

A CHRISTIAN

Shortly after Jackson arrived in Lexington, he pursued his investigation of religion. The Old Dominion village was theologically divided among Baptists, Episcopalians, Methodists, Presbyterians, and Wesleyans. The professor visited all of the sects indiscriminately and analyzed their conflicting doctrines.[18] After a great amount of study, Jackson began to favor the Presbyterian Church. Perhaps the dominant influence for this new religious attitude of the major was Lexington's Presbyterian minister, William S. White. Reverend White and Major Jackson discussed religion often, and they both gained much from each other's company.[19]

It is important to understand that Jackson did not accept all of the Presbyterian theology. This denomination's concepts of predestination and infant baptism were particularly repulsive to him. He had a good knowledge of the Bible and simply could not fit these Presbyterian doctrines into his understanding of the gospel. There were other aspects of this church's doctrine that the professor was uneasy about, and he discussed them thoroughly with the minister.[20]

Jackson felt a need to belong to a denomination but was troubled by the fact that each of them taught principles with which he could not agree. He explained this dilemma to Reverend White, and the minister told him that he could join the Presbyterian Church and continue to work out the reservations that he had. Later the major accepted communion in the Presbyterian Church; but he never found what he would consider to be the completely true church.[21]

Although Jackson had many doctrinal questions, he was always a devout Christian. With deep respect, he followed the minister as a Christian guide. In fact, the professor stated that if he had gained the proper education and power of speech, he would have entered the ministry.[22] Jackson often referred to Reverend White as his "superior officer"[23] and the minister recalled that the major would sometimes "report for orders."[24] This Christian relationship between Jackson and White edified both of them.

Jackson was elected a deacon in the Presbyterian Church on December 26, 1857.[25] He still had many reservations about the doctrine of this church, but he felt that he could serve his Heavenly Father in a church office. As far as the major was concerned, there was no denomination in Lexington at the time that offered an alternative for him. Jackson worked extremely hard in his church job. His main duty was to collect money from the members and distribute it to the poor. In his personal contributions to the church, the professor was generous. He continually donated a tithing, one tenth of his income, to the minister.[26]

One evening there was a deacons' meeting scheduled at the Lexington Presbyterian chapel. The business that the church officers were going to discuss seemed important to Jackson. Of course, the major was in the chapel at the exact hour to take part in the meeting. One of the deacons did not arrive on time, and Jackson paced back and forth with his watch in his hand for five minutes, waiting for the deacon. After this unusual exercise the major left the church building to search for the lost sheep. Jackson went to the man's home and knocked loudly on the door. When the man came to the door Jackson said sharply, "It is eight minutes after 8 [*sic*] o'clock." The man replied, "Yes, Major, I am aware of that, but I didn't have time to go out to-night." "Didn't have time," Jackson shouted.

> Why sir, I should not suppose that you *had time for anything else*. Did we not set apart this hour (only one in the month) for the service of the Church? How then can you put aside your obligations in the matter?[27]

After that startling rebuke the major walked rapidly to the chapel with the negligent deacon following closely behind. Reverend White later recalled that as long as Jackson was a deacon, the minister never worried about the temporal affairs of his congregation.[28]

Jackson developed a great amount of faith during his years in Lexington. Because of his strong conviction, he was able to exercise a high degree of discipline in living by the religious laws. The members of the Presbyterian Church recognized the relationship that the deacon developed with God. Jackson was so devout that many in the congregation felt he was near the spiritual world.[29] The people in the Lexington Church would often question Jackson about his faith. One day one of them asked the deacon to suppose:

> that the providence of God seemed to direct you to drop every scheme of life and of personal advancement, and go on a mission to the heart of Africa for the rest of your days, would you go?

His eyes brightened, and he answered, "I would go *without my hat!*"[30] Thomas also wrote to his sister, Laura, about the growth of his faith:

> Within the past few years I have endeavored to live more nearly unto God. And now nothing earthly could induce me to return to the world again. My life is not one of privation,

37

as you sometimes see among Christians, but I enjoy the pleasures of the world, but endeavor to restrict them within the limits which nature's God has assigned to them. Do you not remember that I told you that I believed that God would restore me to perfect health, and such continues to be my belief . . . For my part, I am willing to go hence when it shall be His great will to terminate my earthly career. Hence you, knowing His will as set forth in His holy word, easily observe how strictly I will adhere to your advice, given some time since; and truly it was good advice, and such as I would not violate to save my head. Yes, my dear sister, rather than willfully violate the known will of God I would forfeit my life; it may seem strange to you, yet nevertheless such a resolution I have taken, and I will by it abide. My daily prayers are for your salvation and some of my prayful petitions have been answered.[31]

Jackson sent many letters containing religious advice to his sister. One of his most interesting messages dealt with temptation:

You speak of your temptations—that you shall be a cast-away [sic]. Don't [sic] tolerate such an idea for a moment. God withdraws His sensible presence from us to try our faith. When a cloud comes between you and the sun, do you fear that the sun will never appear again? I am well satisfied that you are a child of God, and that you will be saved in heaven, then forever to dwell with the ransomed of the Lord. So you must not doubt. The natural sun may never return to the view of the child of God, but the Son of Righteousness will. But there is one very essential thing to the child of God who would enjoy the comforts of religion, and that is he or she must live in accordance with the law of God, must have no will but His; knowing the path of duty must not hesitate for a moment, but at once walk in it. Jesus says, "My yoke is easy and my burden is light," and this is true, if we but follow Him in the prompt discharge of every duty; but we mustn't hesitate a moment about doing our duty, under all circumstances, as soon as it is made known to us; and we should always seek by prayer to be taught our duty.

If temptations are presented, you must not think that you are committing sin in consequence of having a sinful thought. Even the Savior was presented with the thought of worshipping Satan; what could be more abhorrent to a Christian's feelings than such a thought? But such thoughts become sinful if we derive pleasure from them. We must abhor them if we would prevent our sinning. The devil injects sinful ideas into our minds to disturb our peace, and to make us sin; and it is our duty to see by prayer and watchfulness that we are not defiled by them. God has done great things, astonishing things for you and your family. Don't doubt His eternal love for you.[32]

The professor developed a strong power of prayer, which he did not always have. Shortly after Jackson became a member of the Presbyterian Church, Reverend White called on him to pray in a meeting. The major offered such a poor petition and embarrassed himself to such an extent that the minister did not call on him again. After a few weeks Jackson discussed his public prayer with Reverend White. The professor said:

My comfort has nothing in the world to do with it, sir; you as my pastor, think that it is my duty to lead in public prayer—I think so too—and by God's grace I mean to do it. I wish you would please be so good as to call on me more frequently.[33]

The minister complied with this request, and Jackson's ability to pray grew quickly. Later, some of the church members stated that when the professor prayed his whole countenance would change.[34]

Thomas Jackson believed in the biblical injunction to pray always. In a letter to his sister he wrote about how he was able to follow this commandment:

> I have so fixed the habit of prayer to God in my own mind that I never raise a glass of water to my lips without lifting my heart to God in thanks and prayer for the water of life. Then when we take our meals there is grace. Whenever I drop a letter in the post office I send a petition along with it for God's blessing upon its mission and on the person to whom it is sent. When I break on the seal of a letter just received I stop to ask God to prepare me for its contents and make it a messenger of God. When I go to my classroom and await the arrangement of my students, that is my time to intercede with God for them. And so in every act of the day I have made the practice of prayer habitual.[35]

The professor also believed in strict observance of the Sabbath day. He would not travel on Sunday and would not allow a letter of his to be carried on that day. Jackson felt that when he mailed a letter that traveled on Sunday he was forcing the postal employees to break a commandment. Something that caused the major great concern was when a message took more than a week to reach its destination.[36] In reply to a letter from his sister he wrote: "I derive an additional pleasure in reading a letter, resulting from a conviction that it has not been traveling on the Sabbath."[37] One Saturday evening, years later, when war between the North and South seemed imminent, Jackson's wife was distressed about the national situation. He told her:

> My dear, to-morrow is the blessed Sabbath day. It is also the regular communion season at our church. I hope I shall not be called to leave until Monday. Let us then dismiss from our conversation and our thoughts everything pertaining to the war, and have together one more quiet evening of preparation for our loved Sabbath duties.[38]

Jackson's sister, Laura, was not always a Christian, and Thomas felt that it was his duty to help her become one. He reasoned with her in a letter this way:

The best plan that I can conceive for an unbeliever in God, as presented to us in the Bible, is to first consider things with reference merely to expediency. Now considering the subject with reference to expediency only, let us examine whether it is safer to be a Christian or an infidel. Suppose that of two persons, one a Christian, and the other an infidel, [the infidel] is right, and the Christian is wrong; they will then after death be upon an equality. But instead of the infidel being right, suppose him to be wrong, and the Christian right; then will the state of the latter after death be inestimably superior to that of the other. And if you examine the history of mankind, it will be plain that Christianity contributes much more to happiness in this life than that of infidelity. Now having briefly glanced at this subject, to what decision are we forced on the mere ground of expediency; certainly it is to the adoption of Christianity, the next point is to consider whether we can believe the teachings of the *sacred* volume; if so, then its adoption should of necessity follow. I have examined the subject maturely, and the evidence is very conclusive; and if we do not receive the Bible as being authentic and credible, we must reject every other ancient work, as there is no other in favor of which so much evidence can be adduced.[39]

He also sent these lines to her:

It is useless for men to tell me there is no God and that His benign influence is not to be experienced in prayer when it is offered in conformity to the Bible. For some time past not a single day has passed without my feeling His hallowing presence whilst at my morning prayers. I endeavor to live in accordance with the passage "Acknowledge God in all thy ways

41

and He shall direct thy paths" which means, as I understand it, in all thy ways acknowledge God, and He shall take care of you in all respects.[40]

Laura wrote back to Thomas that she would like to please him but if she professed a belief in Christianity at that time she would be a hypocrite. He replied to her:

You must not suppose that I would like to see————profess religion without possessing it. A hypocrite is, in my judgment, one of the most detestable of beings. My opinion is that everyone should honestly and carefully investigate the Bible, and then if he can believe it to be the word of *God* to follow its teachings.[41]

His sister became quite discouraged in her search for faith in Christ, so Thomas told her: "I wrote you this morning that you must not be discouraged. 'All things work together for good.' "[42]

Some time later Laura did profess a belief in Christianity, and this made Thomas happy. He wrote to her:

I thank Heavenly Father for having given you that peace which passeth all understanding, and which the world can neither give nor take away. The world may wrong us and deceive us, but it never can take from us that joy resulting from an assurance of God's love. You may expect dark hours, but never for one moment permit yourself to despond.
The followers of Christ are expressly told in the Bible that in this life they shall have tribulation; but our Savior has told us to be of good cheer, for He has overcome the world; which teaches us that if we but persevere in the ways of well-doing that we also shall overcome the world.[43]

Thomas was undoubtedly one of the most devout Christians to ever set foot on this earth. While he lived in Lexington, a terrible disease was spreading around the home of his sister. She wrote to him expressing concern for her life, and Thomas replied:

> Yours has come safe to hand, and I regret to learn from its contents that death has made such havoc among your neighbors; yet all must pay the same final debt and my sincere desire and thrice daily prayer is, that when your exit comes that your previous preparation will have been made. How *glorious* will it be in that August and heaven-ordained day to meet with mother, brother, sister and father around the shining throne of Omnipotence; there I wish and hope to meet you, with a joy that shall never be alloyed by separation.[44]

On another occasion a friend asked Jackson if he really felt that the line, "All things work together for the good to them that love God," was true. The major said that he believed that it was. The friend then asked, "If you were to lose your health, would you believe it then?" "Yes, I think I should," Jackson replied. "How if you were to become entirely blind?" "I should still believe it," the professor answered. "But suppose, in addition to your loss of health and sight, you should become utterly dependent upon the cold charities of the world?" Jackson paused for a short time and then spoke earnestly: "If it were the will of God to place me there, He would enable me to lie there peacefully a hundred years."[45] Further insight about his feelings on this topic can be gained in reading this line to his sister: "No earthly calamity can shake my hope in the future so long as God is my friend."[46]

BLACK SUNDAY SCHOOL

Jackson was an extremely conscientious man, and this trait can be seen in his treatment of the family slaves. The major was strict with them, but he was also kind. He recognized the need that his black people had to learn the gospel, and so he taught them himself, as some of the slaveholders did at that time. This religious instruction included inviting the servants to family prayers and a special meeting just for the servants on Sunday afternoon. This meeting was found to be so interesting by Jackson's slaves that other blacks learned about it and asked if they could attend. The professor soon realized that if he was going to satisfy the needs of the servants in Lexington, he must organize a Sunday school for them. Such a school was formed by the major in the fall of 1855.[47]

The black Sunday school grew rapidly from a humble beginning. It was supported with Jackson's own money, and he and his wife were the main teachers.[48] Eventually, between eighty and a hundred slaves attended the religious service. With this large number of students the professor found that he needed more teachers, so about twelve of the educated white citizens in Lexington were asked to act as instructors. The expanded faculty was a helpful addition to the school.[49]

The major was an energetic person, and much of his nervous energy was expended on the black Sunday school. He spent a great amount of time each week preparing for the Sunday meeting. Some of his associates noticed that Jackson took his detailed reports about the black Sunday school with him nearly everywhere he went. This enabled the major to work on the reports during his free time and also to show them to anyone who might be interested. He was always concerned about getting as much community support for the school as he could. The professor continued to direct this successful organization until the spring of 1861.[50]

JACKSON'S MINISTER

The influence of Reverend William S. White on Major Thomas J. Jackson was strong.[51] The two men enjoyed each other's company and they spent much time together. Because the reverend had such an impact on the professor, one can learn, to a limited extent, about Jackson's theological beliefs by studying the original writings of White. Most of the original writings of the Presbyterian minister are contained in some manuscripts that were used by him for Sunday-school lessons.

Reverend White felt that it was important for Christians to keep the commandments. In connection with this principle of obedience White borrowed from the Bible, "Seek ye first His kingdom and his righteousness."[52] The minister went on to promise that all things would be added.[53] One of Reverend White's favorite examples used in explanation of this law was Abraham. He wrote that Abraham displayed the virtue of "prompt unquestioning *obedience*."[54] The reverend also referred to the Scribes and Pharisees to demonstrate his point. He paraphrased: "Except *your* righteousness exceed the righteousness of the Scribes and Pharisees ye shall in now wise enter into the kingdom of heaven."[55] For Reverend White there was no double standard; he felt the members must keep all of the commandments written in the holy scriptures.

The minister taught that temptation comes from Satan and trials come from God. White wrote about Christ, "the dispenser of bread,"[56] and how the Savior attained preeminence even "in the gentile world."[57] The reverend recorded that Christ rose above "His persecution, separation from his bretheren"[58] and other hardships to become the Savior of the world. Later he compared Christ to Israel on this topic and wrote:

> She shall be the head of the nations of the earth and not the tail . . . The position which Israel will then hold toward the nations of the earth seems to be foreshadowed in the remarkable blessing pronounced upon the beloved Joseph.[59]

Joseph was another biblical figure used by Reverend White in explaining this principle of progress in overcoming trials. The minister recorded this concerning Joseph:

The spirit with which he bears his own misfortunes brought him into sympathetic touch with the prisoners . . . God illuminated Joseph's mind as He did the prophets.[60]

Joseph was rewarded for his ability to withstand trials, and Reverend White wrote about how this reward might apply to his congregation: "If the motive is 'to be seen of men' the reward will be the approval of men. If the motive is God-conscious, the reward will be from Him."[61]

Reverend White was convinced that men should be instruments in God's hand. The minister recorded this concerning Moses: "Now what God can accomplish, through the 'vast weight of a man' trained and yielding absolutely to His will."[62] He continued, writing:

The wonderful thing is, that through this perfectly natural incident, God gets His instrument sheltered and trained in the palace of Pharaoh himself, the very child he was probably trying to destroy.[63]

White thought that one of Moses' greatest qualities as an instrument of God was that he "never forgot that his people were in bondage and that he was the ordained deliverer."[64] The reverend also used Joseph as an example for this principle:

God had pre-determined (a) to bring Israel out of Caanan into Egypt, and make of them a great nation there . . . (b) Joseph was to be the instrument by which they were to be brought down, received by Pharaoh, and a place made for them in Egypt.[65]

White explained: "The famine was the means of elevating Joseph, bringing Jacob to Egypt, giving Joseph headship over his bretheren . . . "[66] The minister did not use only the figures of Moses and Joseph to express his idea. Many others were referred to. White wrote:

46

God's dependence upon men as instruments of His will, Abraham, Joseph, Moses, Samuel, David, John the Baptist, Jesus Christ, Paul and so on through the ages. Many of these instruments were chosen and ordained before they were born into this world. See Jeremiah 1:4.[67]

Reverend White developed great admiration for Christian soldiers. Few ministers seem to comprehend, as White did, the great sacrifice that men have made for the cause of freedom while serving in the profession of arms. Reverend White wrote about Benjamin and later Judah in connection with this unpleasant but necessary duty:

A tribe of fierce fighters. Skillful with the bow and all left-handed. Saul and Jonathan give us this type of development in this tribe. Mighty fighters, like Saul, the son of Kish, yet with an unusual spiritual insight like Jonathan: for when the Ten Tribes revolt Benjamin stands firm with Judah, a joint guardian of Mount Zion, and in Ezekiel's plan of appointment for redeemed Israel, Judah guards the sacred precincts of the North, while Benjamin stands nearest on the South.[68]

The minister recognized Moses as a great soldier:

God did not keep Moses at the University of On for nothing all these years. He had use for all the wisdom of the Egyptians in the task before him. He became mighty in word, probably a great poet, as afterward shown, and deed [sic]. Josephus says he was a distinguished soldier in the campaign.[69]

Moses and the tribes of Benjamin and Judah were not the only examples that Reverend White used. The voluminous list was given in part in this line:

Certainly both Moses and Joshua, and maybe Caleb, Hur and others, must have had military training and experience in handling large bodies of men.[70]

47

This doctrine concerning commandments, trials, instruments, and soldiers taught by White was a significant part of the religious belief of Jackson. The deacon was extremely conscientious about keeping all of the commandments. He knew the meaning of the word *trial* because his life was one. The professor felt that he was an instrument in God's hand, and he attempted to recognize and perform his mission. Finally, the major was a Christian soldier in every sense of the word.

POOR HEALTH

During the decade that Jackson spent in Lexington, his health continued to bother him. He wrote to his sister: "I am enjoying myself more than I have done for some years, but still my health requires much care and rigid regard to diet."[71] Perhaps the most painful part of his bad health was his eyes. Every time the professor used a candle to study, his eyes would burn with pain. He was continually concerned with the possibility of becoming totally blind.[72] Occasionally, Jackson would notice some improvement in his vision, as this line to his sister suggests: "My eyes are improving but still I have to be careful with them; the spots continue to float before them."[73] The general condition of his eyes is perhaps better expressed in this message, again written to his sister:

> My eyes were so weak some months since that I could not look long at objects through the window; and to look out-of-doors was frequently painful, though but for a moment; and I was reduced to the necessity of masking my looking glass, on account of its reflection. I could not look at a candle, not even for a second without pain.[74]

A final line written by the major about his vision reveals the helplessness of his situation: "I am so thankful to our ever-kind

Heavenly Father for having so improved my eyes as to enable me to write at night. "[75] Of course the professor's poor vision was a continual burden on him in studying for his classes at the Institute. [76]

A problem that seemed to Jackson even more serious than that involving his eyes was his chronic dyspepsia. The professor tried everything that he could think of to cure this illness, but nothing would end it completely. He had many hydropathic treatments at local springs, and this helped to some extent. [77] The major wrote about his hydropathic experiment:

> My health has been much improved by visiting the Alum Springs. I have been and am still using the water, but its effects are not so good as when used at the springs. [78]

It seemed that the trips to the springs helped his attitude toward his physical problem as much as it did his health.

Jackson used other methods in addition to the ones previously mentioned to improve his physical condition. Shortly after he purchased his home in Lexington, the major installed some exercise equipment in it. He used these appliances, along with his regular walks, to get a great amount of exercise. [79] The professor developed other habits resulting from his health condition. He never used tobacco or alcohol while he lived in Lexington. Jackson also avoided tea and coffee for many years. And after he conducted a detailed study of his eating habits, no one could tempt him to eat between meals. [80]

The major's health was such a chronic problem that it had a significant impact on his entire life. Many of his peculiar habits, which the people of Lexington found so amusing, were a direct result of his physical condition. In fact, Jackson's decision to resign his regular army commission and become a professor at the Virginia Military Institute was a direct result of his painful eyes. [81] However, in many ways, the professor used his health condition to great advantage. His strict diet

49

and strenuous exercise helped him to develop a strong body.[82] At night Jackson could not read because of his eyes, so he studied mentally. During this decade of periodic meditation, the professor developed an enormous capacity to concentrate and meditate. The major, who refused to become discouraged, literally turned a curse into blessing.[83]

A PECULIAR MAN

It did not take long for the people in Lexington to decide that Jackson was a peculiar professor. His appearance gave them the first sign of oddness. He was an extremely clumsy man because of his huge feet. Each time the major took a step, he resembled a duck waddling into a pond.[84] However, the citizens in the small Virginia town did not often see the professor. He was usually working at something and removed from the social life of the community. This secluded action reflected Jackson's obsession with the idea of using his ability to the fullest.[85]

There were many ways in which the professor attempted to improve himself. He realized that he was a poor speaker, so he joined a debating group called the Franklin. The major's first few visits to this society closely resembled the experience he had had in the Presbyterian church with prayer. But Jackson would never give up, and eventually he began to speak quite well.[86] Reference has been made previously to the professor's study meditations, and this aspect of his life-style in Lexington cannot be overemphasized. It had an enormous impact on the major's later life.[87] During the daylight hours, Jackson was an avid reader. The Institute had a large library and he read many of the books, particularly about the campaigns of Napoleon.[88]

It is interesting to study Jackson's personality during the time he spent in Lexington. There was no man in the village who was more conscientious. He carried this trait to a point far beyond moderation, but he did it in a humble way. The professor did not consider himself to be an example, and he usually avoided forcing his convictions on his associates.[89]

Some other aspects of Jackson's character come to light during this decade. He never had a great love or interest for people. If someone intentionally lied to the professor, this only served to magnify his distrust. He would totally avoid a person who acted in this manner from that point on.[90] Jackson was a quiet man. He usually felt out of place at parties and other social occasions. This trait had stayed with him since his days at West Point and left him with few close friends.[91]

The major experienced a continual conflict in his character. At times he was ruthless, and on other occasions he was extremely sensitive. Jackson's ruthlessness was probably a reflection of his military training and experience in the Mexican War. However, a female acquaintance of the professor stated:

> Jackson's organism was of a singularly sensitive character . . . His revulsion at scenes of horror, or even descriptions of them, was almost inconsistent in one who had lived the life of a soldier.[92]

Jackson was always kind to small children and elderly people. Some felt that he acted in an almost feminine manner around these two age groups.[93]

The major rarely had any mental conflict when setting priorities in his life. In the spring of 1859 his wife became ill, and he decided to take her to New York in order to obtain the best medical care. Mrs. Jackson stayed in the hospital for many weeks, but the professor returned to his duties at the Institute.[94] Finally, Jackson's wife recovered and wanted to return home. She wrote to him and asked how she should travel to Lexington. The major replied: "In answer to your question how you are to come, I should say, with your husband, if no other arrangements can be effected."[95] He had an obligation at the Institute and duty always came first. His wife returned home alone. Jackson's actions later in the decade, on the eve of the Civil War, are revealing. Americans in all sections of the country could sense the seriousness of the situation. Undoubtedly, the major felt it also, but he never displayed concern about the national political problem. He had faith that God's will would be done. Therefore, although Jackson prayed that war might not occur, he did not worry about the possibility.[96]

There are many lines that can be written to summarize the professor's personality in Lexington during the 1850s. He was a rigid, sincere man and often eccentric in his actions. Much of the time the major worked alone, and this fact never seemed to bother him. Throughout the decade, his sense of duty to God and country was beyond normal comprehension.[97] While walking on the streets of Lexington, the professor often wore an absent look on his face. He would walk down the streets of the little town totally involved in deep thought.[98] No one except Jackson felt that he would ever amount to anything. He was always quiet, so people thought the major must not know anything worthy of conversation. Because the professor worked relentlessly, they were certain that he had no common sense. When he spoke to them, which was rare, his sentences were short and of simple construction. To the citizens of Lexington, this indicated a lack of intellect. His humble attitude kept him from the center of attention whenever he participated in a social activity. If one asked a person in the small village about Major Jackson, he would probably be told that old Tom fool Jackson was an odd man, a religious fanatic, and a complete failure.[99]

NOTES

1. Henderson, pp. 57–58.
2. Dabney, p. 62.
3. Jackson, p. 81.
4. Cooke, p. 24.
5. Dabney, pp. 63–64.
6. Cooke, p. 32.
7. Ibid. p. 17.
8. Dabney, p. 65.
9. Ibid. p. 64.
10. William Couper, *One Hundred Years of Virginia Military Institute*, vol. 1 (Richmond: Garrett and Massie Company, 1939), p. 263.
11. Couper, Vol. III, p. 187.
12. Henderson, pp. 68–69.
13. Dabney, p. 95.
14. Jackson, p. 118.
15. Ibid. p. 120.
16. Ibid. p. 121.
17. Henderson, p. 71.
18. Dabney, p. 83.
19. Jackson, p. 58.
20. Offill, p. 51.
21. Jackson, p. 58.
22. Ibid. pp. 59–60.
24. Ibid.
23. Jones, p. 85.
25. Dabney, pp. 96–97.
26. John O. Casler, *Four Years in the Stonewall Brigade* (Dayton: Morningside Bookshop, 1971), p. 61.
27. Jones, pp. 84–85.
28. Ibid.
29. Henderson, pp. 71–72.
30. Jackson, p. 72.
31. Arnold, pp. 159–160.
32. Jackson to sister, Laura, September 6, 1861, Jackson Collection.
33. Jones, p. 84.
34. Dabney, p. 103.
35. Mary Anna Jackson, *The Life and Letters of General Thomas J. Jackson* (New York: Harper Brothers, 1892), p. 73.
36. Jackson to sister, Laura, June 6, 1856, Jackson Collection.
37. Dabney, p. 641.
38. Jones, p. 86.
39. Arnold, pp. 180–181.
40. Jackson to sister, Laura, February 1, 1853, Jackson Collection.

41. Arnold, pp. 168–169.
42. Dabney, p. 123.
43. Arnold, p. 260.
44. Jackson to sister, Laura, March 1, 1849, Jackson Collection.
45. Jones, p. 90.
46. Arnold, p. 182.
47. Jones, p. 85.
48. Henderson, p. 61.
49. Dabney, p. 93.
50. Jones, p. 87.
51. Jackson, *Memoirs*, p. 59.
52. Williams S. White, papers, Sunday-school lessons. Sunday-school lesson on the commandments. Special Collections, McCormic Library, Washington and Lee University, Lexington, Virginia. Hereafter referred to as White Collection.
53. Ibid.
54. Ibid.
55. Ibid.
56. Ibid., Sunday-School lesson on trials, White Collection.
57. Ibid.
58. Ibid.
59. Ibid.
60. Ibid.
61. Ibid.
62. Ibid., Sunday-school lesson on instruments, White Collection.
63. Ibid.
64. Ibid.
65. Ibid.
66. Ibid.
67. Ibid.
68. Ibid., Sunday-school lesson on Christian soldiers, White Collection.
69. Ibid.
70. Ibid.
71. Arnold, p. 168.
72. Dabney, p. 65.
73. Arnold, p. 220.
74. Ibid. p. 155.
75. Jackson, *Memoirs*, p. 363.
76. Arnold, p. 153.
77. Jackson, *Memoirs*, p. 71.
78. Arnold, p. 191.
79. Jackson, *Memoirs*, p. 72.
80. Henderson, p. 60.
81. Jackson, *Memoirs*, p. 56.
82. Ibid. p. 72.

83. Henderson, pp. 68–69.
84. Cooke, p. 23.
85. Arnold, p. 122.
86. Jackson, *Memoirs*, p. 62.
87. Dabney, p. 67.
88. Henderson, p. 58.
89. Jackson, *Memoirs*, p. 69.
90. Ibid. p. 70.
91. Henderson, p. 60.
92. Arnold, p. 318.
93. Henderson, p. 67.
94. Jackson, *Memoirs*, p. 121.
95. Ibid. p. 135.
96. Ibid. p. 141.
97. Cooke, p. 37.
98. Ibid p. 26.
99. Henderson, p. 63.

CHAPTER SIX

Confederate Army, 1861–1863

If the Valley is lost, Virginia is lost.
Thomas J. Jackson

CHRISTIAN SOLDIER

One Sunday morning a telegram from Governor John Letcher arrived in Lexington for Major Thomas Jackson. It was an order requesting the major to march upper-class cadets of the Virginia Military Institute to Richmond. They were needed at the Old Dominion capital to serve as drillmasters for the Confederate Army. After reading the message, Jackson left home without eating breakfast and walked quickly to the Institute to begin preparations for the march.[1] The professor did not forget that it was the Sabbath, even during this time of emergency. Major Jackson asked that Reverend White come to the military school and hold a religious service shortly before the unit departed. The officer told the minister that the cadets would march promptly at one o'clock. And because the reverend knew Jackson well, he finished the service fifteen minutes early.[2]

After the major had served in Richmond for a short time, he was given command of the Confederate troops at Harpers

Ferry. It is interesting to study the method Jackson used in choosing his staff for this tour of duty because he always did it the same way. He wrote to his wife about the selection:

> My desire, under the direction and blessing of our Heavenly Father, is to get a staff especially qualified for their specific duties, and that will, under the blessing of the Most High, render the greatest possible amount of service to their country.[3]

Some of Jackson's friends wanted him to give them a staff appointment, but they did not receive one. The commander wanted only the best men, so he was very selective.[4] His process of choosing was a detailed one. Jackson would always find out if the prospective staff member was intelligent, dependable, and energetic. The commander's most important question concerned the hour that the man rose in the morning. If any of these requirements were lacking in a candidate, he was promptly rejected.[5]

Jackson earned the name "Stonewall" at the battle of First Manassas. During the fighting General Barnard E. Bee, of the Confederacy, decided to pull back his troops and make another stand at a place called Henry House. While the movement was conducted, the situation for the South began to appear quite desperate. General Bee felt that he might have made a tactical error and he rode a short distance to discuss his position with Jackson, who was also in the area with his troops.[6] Bee exclaimed, "General, they are beating us back." Jackson turned slowly on his horse and replied, "Sir, we'll give them the bayonet."[7] After this brief, inspiring conversation, Bee rode back to his troops and shouted:

> Look yonder! There is Jackson and his brigade standing like a stone wall. Let us determine to die here and we will conquer. Rally behind them![8]

57

After Bee had finished the last sentence, he was shot by a Union bullet. The general died but the name Stonewall did not.[9]

During the first winter of the Civil War, Jackson's troops camped in the Valley of Virginia. General William W. Loring, a subordinate of Jackson, was ordered to post his unit near Romney.[10] Loring did not like his assigned position so he complained to the secretary of war, J.P. Benjamin. Near the end of January, Jackson received this telegram from Benjamin: "Our news indicates that a movement is making to cut off General Loring's command, order him back to Winchester immediately."[11] This order was given to the general without consultation and also without using the chain of command.[12] Jackson sent a message back to Benjamin on the same day:

> Sir,—your order requiring me to direct General Loring to return with his command to Winchester has been received and promptly complied with. With such interference in my command, I cannot expect to be of much service in the field, and I accordingly respectfully request to be ordered to report for duty to the Superintendent of the Virginia Military Institute at Lexington, as has been done in the case of other professors. Should this application not be granted, I respectfully request that the President will accept my resignation from the army.[13]

Some of the general's staff members explained to him that the government had probably made a mistake and he replied: "Certainly they have; but they must be taught not to act so hastily without a full knowledge of the facts."[14] Finally, Governor Letcher convinced General Jackson that he should withdraw his resignation.[15]

No general in the South was more determined than Stonewall Jackson. Much of the time twenty percent of his army was without shoes, fifty percent of them wore rags for clothes, and all of the corps were poorly fed.[16] The commander continually attempted to solve the logistical problems, but he fought as if they already were solved. His "foot cavalry"[17] engaged in many long, rapid marches. Every minute was important to the general, and so his rules of march were dynamic.[18] It was not unusual for his troops to move fifty miles in two days and capture most of their supplies from the enemy on the way.[19]

The Confederate soldiers learned to admire Jackson for his inexhaustible energy and ability to hold ground when necessary.[20] Once a subordinate reported to the commander and told him that it was impossible for his men to hold their position. Jackson replied sharply: "You must hold it, my men sometimes fail to drive the enemy, but the enemy always fails to drive my men."[21] On another occasion General Jackson was riding with General Robert E. Lee while a fierce battle was taking place in a nearby forest. General Lee said, "That fire is very heavy! Do you think your men can stand it?" General Jackson replied briefly, "They can stand almost anything. They can stand that!"[22]

One day Jackson met a subordinate, General Richard B. Garnett, with his troops stopped on the side of the road. The commander asked why they had stopped without his order and the officer replied, "I have halted to let the men cook rations." "There is no time for that," Jackson shouted. Garnett exclaimed, "But it is impossible for the men to march further without them!" Jackson remarked bluntly, "I never found anything impossible with that brigade!"[23] On one occasion a colonel halted his men without orders; and, again, Jackson noticed the unit. Jackson asked, "Colonel, why do you not get your brigade together, keep it together and move on?" The colonel replied, "It's impossible, General; I can't do it." Jackson then shouted:

Don't say it's impossible. Turn your command over to the next officer. If he can't do it, I'll find someone who can, if I have to take him from the ranks![24]

A final example demonstrates how totally determined Jackson was. At Malvern Hill a unit commander received an order from Jackson that was so dangerous he could not believe it. He returned from his position and asked Jackson, "Did you order me to advance over that field, sir?" "Yes," was the reply. The subordinate officer said excitedly: "Impossible, sir! My men will be annihilated! Nothing can live there! They will be annihilated!" Jackson said nothing for a few minutes. Then he raised his hand and said: "General————,I always endeavor to take care of my wounded and to bury my dead. You have heard my order—obey it!"[25]

Stonewall Jackson's men realized that he was not a completely ruthless and egotistical commander. Many times as they marched swiftly to the front, the general would sit nearby on his horse with his right hand raised straight in the air and his head bowed in prayer.[26] This inspired the soldiers to unsurpassed feats of bravery. They knew that "by the sweat of their brow, he was saving their blood."[27]

One of the general's favorite commands was to march at "early dawn."[28] He insisted that his staff always ride near the front of the army. Some of the members complained, but none of them ever changed Jackson's mind.[29] The marches during the day were long and rapid. The commander found it much more difficult to decide when to retire than when to rise.[30] On many nights he was working at 2:00 A.M. to make preparations for the next day.[31] One of his staff members wrote:

For a while I was wont to wonder if the General ever slept, but I soon found out that he did sleep a great deal, often at odd times. If he had just five minutes to spare for the recreation he could sleep four and a half minutes of it and be wide awake when the five minutes was up.[32]

People never ceased to be amazed at the way this odd-looking character led his troops.[33] Jackson was usually exhausted, so he rode his horse in an amusing manner, leaning toward the front of his saddle most of the time. It appeared that the general did not realize he was on his horse.[34] Jackson did not pay much attention to his personal appearance, which was homely to begin with. His uniforms were usually old and his cap was faded. The commander's face often reflected the fact that his thoughts were far from where he was. He rode along, quietly planning an invasion of the North or mentally toying with some other strategy.[35]

This quiet, unassuming man caused fear to envelope the Union troops when he marched his soldiers toward them. One day a Federal unit was camped at Romney, and Jackson decided to capture the town. The Confederate Army advanced toward the village and was about a day's march away when the Union officers learned of the distant threat. The United States troops were greater in number and also well positioned, but they had such a fear of Jackson's soldiers that they left Romney without their tents and some other equipment.[36] Later at Harpers Ferry a Northern prisoner of war commented with reference to Jackson: "Boys, he's not much for looks, but if we'd had him we wouldn't have been caught in this trap."[37] The other Union prisoners around him voiced their approval of his statement.[38] A Federal officer once commented, "Stonewall Jackson's men will follow him to the devil and he knows it."[39] And, on another occasion, a Union surgeon exclaimed:

If Stonewall Jackson ever gets so completely surrounded that he cannot march or fight his way out he will take wings unto himself and his army and fly out.[40]

The general felt that mystery was "the secret of success,"[41] and he adhered to this principle throughout his military career.[42] Once an officer asked, "General, where are you going?" "Can you keep a secret?" Jackson replied. "Yes," said the officer. "Ah, so can I."[43] All that Jackson's troops usually knew about where they were going was that it was "somewhere."[44] General James Longstreet's army was amused with Jackson's secrecy and often referred to his unit as the "lost" corps.[45] Jackson's own men did not seem to be bothered by their commander's secrecy. This is reflected in a statement by one of his soldiers:

> Military men don't tell privates their plans, and General Jackson never told officers his. But we knew it was all right when "Old Bluelight" gave his orders. We found out afterwards the cause.[46]

The general never discussed his goals and rarely asked for advice.[47] He also did much of the reconnaissance by himself.[48] Jackson was a quiet man and his emotions were not dynamic. His servant, Jim, recalled that the only way that he could tell if something was going to happen was when the general got up in the night to pray. Jackson's prayers in the night were a signal for Jim to get things packed, "Cos den I knowed dere wuz a move on hand."[49]

The commander was such a peculiar person that many people thought he was promoted far beyond his ability. The Southern newspapers often printed relatively short articles about his military success. This did not bother Jackson, but it did concern his wife. In reply to her letters he wrote:

> You think that the papers ought to say more about me. My brigade is not a brigade of newspaper correspondents. I know that the 1st Brigade was the first to meet and pass our retreating forces, to push on with no other aid than the smiles of God, to boldly take its position with the artillery that was under my command, to arrest the victorious foe in his own progress, to

hold him in check until reinforcements arrived, and, finally to charge bayonets, and thus advancing, pierce the enemy's center.[50]

On another occasion he comforted her by writing:

Don't trouble yourself about representations that are made of me. These things are earthly and transitory. There are real and glorious blessings, I trust, in reserve for us, beyond this life. It is best for us to keep our eyes fixed upon the throne of God, and the realities of a more glorious existence beyond the verge of time. It is gratifying to be beloved, and to have our conduct approved by our fellow men; but this is not worthy to be compared with the glory that is in reservation for us in the presence of the glorified Redeemer. Let us endeavor to adorn the doctrine of Christ our Savior, in all things; knowing that there awaits us "a far more exceeding and eternal weight of glory." I would not relinquish the slightest diminution of that glory, for all this world, and all that it can give. My prayer is, that such may ever be the feeling of my heart.[51]

The general's wife was continually asking him to take a furlough and come home to visit her. At Christmas time in 1862 he replied to her request:

It appears to me, that it is better for me to remain with my command so long as the war continues, if our ever gracious Heavenly Father permit. The army suffers immensely by absentees. If all our troops, officers and men, were at their posts, we might, through God's blessing, expect a more speedy termination of the war. The temporal affairs of some are so deranged as to make a strong plea for their returning home for a short time, but *our God* has greatly blessed me and mine during my absence; and whilst it would be a great comfort to see you, and our darling little daughter, and others in whom I take special interest, yet duty appears to require me to remain

63

with my command. It is important that those at head-quarters set an example by remaining at the post of duty.[52]

A short time later he answered her in a letter:

You want to know whether I could get a furlough. My darling, I can't be absent from my command, as my attention is necessary in preparing my troops for hard fighting should it be required; and as my officers and soldiers are not permitted to go and see their wives and families, I ought not to see my *esposita,* as it might make the troops feel that they were badly treated, and that I consult my own pleasure and comfort regardless of theirs: so you had better stay at cottage home for the present, as I do not know how long I shall remain here.[53]

Jackson's wife was, in many ways, as persistent as the general, and she came to visit him in the field. Mrs. Jackson later wrote about the experience:

It was my good fortune to find an escort to the army, and I joyfully set out, in compliance with my husband's somewhat doubtful permission, to pay him a visit. . . . [54]
All was quiet in the army during my visit, and although my husband was unremitting in his duties to his command, yet he had sufficient leisure to devote to my pleasure to make the time pass most delightfully.[55]

As one can perceive from the above quotations, Jackson was extremely devoted to duty. During the entire time that he served in the Confederate Army he never requested a furlough and was never away from his command for even a day.[56]

There are many stories that have been written about Jackson and his service in the Confederate Army. One day the general's corps was marching to battle near Malvern Hill. The commander was about a mile behind the front lines and sitting under a tree writing an order. The troops were marching on a road close to him. It was dry, so there was a large cloud of dust. Union artillerymen observed the cloud and opened fire on it. The incoming shells killed about six men, and dirt was thrown all over the general. Without looking up, he continued to write. After Jackson had finished the message, he stood up and told the soldiers to take care of the casualties.

Then he rode casually off to the battle front.[57] On one occasion Jackson was attending a council of war that concerned some significant strategic decisions. After he heard all of the others speak, the general requested that he be given the opportunity to share his opinion the next morning. This appeal was granted, and as the Confederate generals were leaving the room, A. P. Hill said to Richard S. Ewell, "Well! I suppose Jackson wants time to pray over it!"[58] Some time after the conference, Ewell needed to see Jackson about another matter. When he reached Stonewall's tent, Ewell found the Christian on his knees in earnest prayer. As Ewell listened to Jackson's plea to God, he was deeply moved and remarked after the visit, "If that is religion, I must have it."[59] Ewell became a Christian in a few weeks and attributed his conversion to the humble prayer of Jackson.[60]

Stonewall Jackson was a busy man, but he occasionally found time to visit the Confederate hospitals. During one of his tours a young girl recognized the general. The girl was so impressed with the reputation of the Confederate officer, that she asked one of his aids if she could give him a kiss. The aid transfered the message to the commander and his reaction was interesting. Jackson was so embarrassed that he blushed and moved away with a muffled laugh. The courageous battle leader was completely confused in this situation.[61]

A Presbyterian minister came to visit the general in 1861. The reverend was soon exposed to many humorous stories about Jackson. A close associate of the general said to the minister:

The truth is, sir, that Old Jack is *crazy*. I can account for his conduct in no other way. Why, I frequently meet him out in the woods walking back and forth muttering to himself incoherent sentences and gesticulating wildly, and at such times he seems utterly oblivious of my presence and of everything else.[62]

Later the minister had an opportunity to speak with General Jackson about the incidents, and the reverend heard this explanation from the commander:

I find that it greatly helps me in fixing my mind and quickening my devotion to give articulate utterance to my prayers, and hence I am in the habit of going off into the woods, where I can be alone and speak audibly to myself the prayers I would pour out to my God. I was at first annoyed that I was compelled to keep my eyes open to avoid running against the trees and stumps; but upon investigating the matter I do not find that scriptures require us to close our eyes in prayer, and the exercise has proven to me very delightful and profitable.[63]

One time Jackson's corps was camped near Richmond and so the general used the opportunity to attend church on Sunday. It was the first time that the commander had been in the capital for this purpose. He entered one of the chapels without a military aid and humbly took a seat near the back of the building. During the service he was extremely attentive, and when the meeting ended, the general left quickly. Most of the people at the religious gathering did not even know that Stonewall Jackson had been there.[64]

The general rarely read a newspaper, and seemed to be almost totally unconcerned about his public image. Jackson was simply too busy directing his corps to worry about what people thought of him. However, one day Captain Alexander Pendleton read to the staff some lines from *The New York Mercury*. The commander sat back in his chair and listened closely. A smile began to spread over Jackson's face and he was apparently enjoying the story. When the captain finished the article, the general could not contain himself any longer and started to laugh more loudly than the staff had ever heard him laugh before. An officer later commented that this was "the only time I ever heard him listen to what the press had to say about him."[65]

It is difficult to comprehend the great amount of work that Jackson did as a general. After capturing Harpers Ferry, the Confederate commander had to discuss terms of surrender with General Julius White, the defeated Union commander. In an informal meeting, a Southern aid introduced the two officers: "General, this is General White, of the United States Army." Jackson attempted to act in a respectful manner but was so exhausted that he nearly fell asleep. The aid continued: "He has come to arrange the terms of surrender!" Jackson did not react to this sentence, so the subordinate officer looked under the general's hat. He found him sound asleep. He woke the general up, and finally Jackson said, in a strained voice, "The surrender must be unconditional, General. Every indulgence can be granted afterwards." Following this short statement, Jackson's head nodded and the conversation was over.[66]

The people in Lexington became more interested in the general as the war continued. After each battle they met at the local post office to hear the latest news. One day Reverend White was among the crowd and received a personal letter from Jackson. The minister exclaimed, "Now we will have the news!"[67] All of the citizens moved in closely to hear the message from their hero, but they were greatly disappointed. The letter did not have a line about the last victory. It only contained a check for fifty dollars to help the black Sunday school purchase books and some questions about the condition of the school and church.[68]

On one occasion, while Jackson was waiting in the rear

67

of his command during a fierce battle, a member of his staff handed him a drawing of Captain Dabney Carr Harrison, a Presbyterian minister killed at Fort Donelson. The general thanked the officer for giving him the picture and then started a long discussion about the power of example. A messenger rode up swiftly and shouted, "The enemy advancing." Jackson replied simply, "Open on them,"[69] and then continued the religious discussion. The conversation went on for a long time and the general was interrupted only to receive messages and give orders.[70]

The commander often rode with his staff, and one day after a battle they were moving to another position. During the trip, Jackson noticed a persimmon tree with a large amount of fruit. It was one of his favorite foods, so he dismounted and climbed the tree to satisfy his appetite. For some time he remained in the tree and quietly ate the delicious fruit. After he had eaten all that he wanted, the general started to get out of the tree. However, he soon found that it was easier to climb up than it was to climb down, and the clumsy commander became hopelessly stranded in the small tree. The staff observed his helpless condition and learned that he could not move up or down. With all of the general's subordinates on the verge of laughter, they found some planks in a fence and helped him slide to the ground. This story was not published in the Southern newspapers; but it is true, nevertheless.[71]

Stonewall Jackson enjoyed prayer, occasionally for extended periods of time. One evening a member of his staff entered the general's tent and found him on his knees. The young major waited for a half an hour, and then left to ask an aide if the commander had fallen asleep in that position because of too much work. The aid quickly replied, "Oh no; you know the general is an old Presbyterian and they all make long prayers."[72] The staff member went back to Jackson's tent and after about an hour the general got up and spoke with the major.[73]

Jackson felt there was a close connection between Christianity and the military. He talked with his chaplain, Reverend B.T. Lacy, many times about the topic, and one time the general said, in reference to faith in God:

In the commander of an army at the critical hour, it calms his perplexities, moderates his anxieties, steadies the scales of judgement, and thus preserves him from exaggerated and rash conclusions.[74]

On another occasion, General Jackson turned to a staff member, Lieutenant James P. Smith, and said with a smile, "Can you tell me where the Bible gives generals a model for their official reports of battles?" The lieutenant replied that he had never thought of looking there. The general continued:

Nevertheless, there are such; and excellent models, too. Look, for instance, at the narrative of Joshua's battle with the Amalekites; there you have one. It has clearness, brevity, fairness, modesty; and it traces the victory to its right source—the blessing of God.[75]

As military historians look back at the service of Stonewall Jackson in the Confederate Army, and particularly his famous Valley Campaign, they are amazed at what he was able to do. One scholar summarized Jackson's military success in the Valley of Virginia this way:

In thirty days his army had marched nearly four hundred miles, skirmishing almost daily, fought five battles, defeated four armies, two of which were completely routed, captured about twenty pieces of artillery, some four thousand prisoners, and immense quantity of stores of all kinds, and had done all this with a loss of less than one thousand killed, wounded and missing. Surely a more brilliant record cannot be found in the history of the world, and General Jackson might well say this was accomplished "through God's blessing."[76]

CHAPLAINS

The chaplains in Jackson's corps worked hard because of the commander's interest in their duties. After each victory the general would publish an order encouraging the soldiers to attend a " 'Thanksgiving' Service."[77] The religious meetings were particularly large following the battles with General Nathaniel P. Banks at Winchester and with General John C. Fremont at Strasburg. However, after every engagement with the enemy Jackson's "foot cavalry"[78] seemed eager to worship their God.[79]

The general enjoyed talking with his chaplains about the religious activity of the army and other theological topics. One night shortly before the Battle of Fredericksburg, a chaplain noticed an officer covered with a blanket so that his rank could not be seen. The soldier was resting just behind a battery and reading the Bible, so the minister decided to start a conversation with him. The reverend began by talking about the imminent conflict against the enemy, but the officer soon changed the subject to religious matters. The conversation became so deeply theological in nature that the minister asked the officer, "What regiment are you chaplain of?"[80] To the reverend's surprise the student of scriptures was Stonewall Jackson.[81]

Another chaplain related a conversation that he had with the commander. The discussion included topics such as devotion to God, missionary work in the corps, and chaplains in the army. Jackson freely expressed his views, and the minister learned a great deal. In fact, the chaplain later stated that "I had to lay aside my office as teacher in Israel"[82] and listen to the excellent instruction from the general. [83]

On one occasion a chaplain in Jackson's corps was walking to a religious meeting at Hamilton's Crossing. During his trip, the general rode by and asked the minister about his destination. After a short conversation Jackson got off his horse and walked with the religious officer. They traveled together for miles in a deep discussion about the religious welfare of the corps and ways to improve it.[84]

On another occasion a chaplain reported to Jackson as the general was on his way to a worship service. The commander invited the officer to go with him and the chaplain accepted. The minister later wrote that he would

> never forget the power, comprehensiveness, and tender pathos of the prayer he made during that delightful prayer-meeting [*sic*].[85]

The chaplain left the commander after receiving a tremendous spiritual uplift.[86]

One of Jackson's religious goals in connection with his corps was to obtain Reverend B.T. Lacy as his chief of chaplains. The general wrote to the leadership of the Presbyterian Church:

> Whilst I hope to have Mr. L. in my *corps*, yet if you think that our church in making a proper distribution of her ministerial talent and piety, can send to my corps another of the gifted sons, I will be greatly gratified, and will contribute to his support as promised in my letter to Colonel Preston.[87]

Reverend Lacy was a general chaplain in the Confederate Army and highly sought after by many of the Southern commanders. However, the chaplain was ordered to serve under Jackson, and the two men worked well together.[88]

When Reverend Lacy arrived at Jackson's headquarters the commander said:

> You are more than welcome to my camp, and it will give me great pleasure to help you in your work in every way in my power. I am more anxious than I can express that my men should be not only good soldiers of their country, but also good soldiers of the cross.[89]

Later the general wrote some words of advice to his chaplain and expressed an evangelical feeling:

> My views are summed up in these few words: each Christian branch of the Church should send into the army some of its most prominent ministers who are distinguished for their piety, talents and zeal. Such ministers should labor to produce concert of action among chaplains and Christians in the army. These ministers should give special attention to preaching to those regiments without chaplains, and let the regiments name the denomination from which they desire chaplains selected and then see that suitable chaplains are selected . . . Denominational distinctions should be kept out of view and not touched upon; as a general rule I do not think that a chaplain who would preach denominational sermons should be in the army. Let not the question be asked as to what denomination does he belong but "does he preach the Gospel?"[90]

Meetings in Jackson's corps were held each week for the chaplains to discuss their theological goals.[91] The commander often met with them and gave the religious leaders his advice. Jackson admonished the ministers "to endure hardness as good soldiers of Jesus Christ."[92] By this statement he meant that they should live with the foot soldiers and gain empathy for them by experiencing all their hardships.[93] This admonition was probably not eagerly accepted by the chaplains, but they followed it, nevertheless. In fact, the meetings were a great success, and much good was accomplished as a result of them.

Many improvements were made in the religious condition of Jackson's corps after Reverend Lacy reported for duty. Each Sunday a chaplain would come to headquarters and hold a meeting for the staff.[94] According to the general, these services proved to be extremely beneficial. During the winter, Jackson's troops were encouraged to build chapels for their religious meetings. Because of this services became more denominational in nature, and this was welcomed by the troops.

Each soldier, no matter what his denomination, felt important and cared for.[95] The commander rarely read newspapers; but, with his approval, a religious publication was established in the corps. This paper enhanced greatly the spiritual welfare of the men.[96] Perhaps more important than the theological innovations themselves was the fact that the changes served as an example for other Southern armies. Before long many of the generals took about as much interest in the religious welfare of their men as Jackson did.[97]

RELIGIOUS CORRESPONDENCE

Jackson never requested or accepted a furlough during his tour of duty in the Confederate Army. As a result of this fact, he wrote many letters in addition to his military communication, and much of this correspondence was of a highly religious nature. The former professor was concerned about the welfare of his slaves, and shortly after leaving Lexington he sent these lines to a friend:

> I am much obliged for your kind letter of the 19th, and for the arrangement respecting Amy and Emma (slaves owned by Jackson). Please have the kindness to go to Winny Bucks occasionally and see that Amy is well cared for, and that not only she but also Emma, is well clothed. I am under special obligations for the religious instruction you have given Amy, and hope that it may be in your power to continue it.[98]

The general wanted his wife to handle the family affairs, with the exception of the slaves, and so he wrote to her about some financial matters on November 9, 1861:

> I think that, as far as possible, persons should take Confederate State Bonds, so as to relieve the government from any pecuniary pressure. You had better not sell your coupon from the bonds, as I understand they are paid in gold, but let the Confederacy keep the gold.[99]

Many of the commander's orders contained direct reference to spiritual topics. After one battle Jackson wrote:

> The Major General Commanding invites you to observe tomorrow evening, June 14th, from 3 [sic] o'clock p.m., as a season of thanksgiving by suspension of all military exercises and by holding divine service in the several regiments.[100]

According to the general this "season of thanksgiving"[101] was "for the purpose of rendering thanks to God for having crowned our arms with success and to implore his continued favor."[102] Jackson's correspondence was often short and to the point. On one occasion he sent a message to the Confederate Government at Richmond that contained only this: "God blessed our arms with victory at McDowell yesterday."[103] The commander published an order in connection with this brief message:

> Soldiers of the Army of the Valley and North West: I congratulate you on your recent victory at M'Dowell [sic]. I request you to unite with me, this morning, in thanksgivings to Almighty God, for thus having crowned your arms with success; and in praying that He will continue to lead you on from victory to victory, until our independence shall be established; and make us that people whose God is the Lord. The Chaplains will hold divine service at 10 o'clock a.m., this day, in their respective regiments.[104]

Jackson circulated a similar order after fighting near Winchester, and the following lines are a portion of it:

> But his chief duty today, and that of the army, is to recognize devoutly the hand of a protecting Providence in the brilliant successes of the last three days, which have given us the results of a great victory without great losses, and to make the obligation of our thanks to God for his mercies to us and our country in heartfelt acts of religious worship. For this purpose the troops will remain in camp to-day, suspending, as far as prac-

ticable, all military exercises, and the chaplains of regiments will hold Divine [sic] services in their several charges at 4 [sic] o'clock p.m. today.[105]

Jackson gave special recognition to God in much of his correspondence. After the conflict of First Manassas he sent this message to his wife:

My precious Pet,—yesterday we fought a great battle and gained a great victory, for which all the glory is due to *God alone*.[106]

The commander wrote this in an official report of his campaigns:

For these great and signal victories, our sincere and humble thanks are due unto almighty God. We should in all things acknowledge the hand of Him who reigns in Heaven, and rules among the armies of men.[107]

In a letter to his wife, Jackson expressed his excitement about the religious activity in his corps:

I trust that God is going to bless us with great success, and in such a manner as to show that it is all His gift; and I trust and pray that it will lead our country to acknowledge Him, and to live in accordance with His will as revealed in the Bible, there appears to be an increased religious interest among our troops here. Our chaplains have weekly meetings on Tuesdays: and the one this week was more charming than the preceeding one.[108]

The general was sincere in his feeling that the Confederate Government should follow Christian principles. In some lines to a friend Jackson wrote: "Let our Government [sic] acknowledge the God of the Bible as its God, and we may expect to be a happy and independent people."[109] After a battle at

Kernstown, Jackson sent this message to his wife:

Our gallant little army is increasing in numbers, and my prayer is that it may be an army of *the living God,* as well as of its country. [110]

It is difficult to comprehend the importance that the commander placed in the power of prayer. With reference to a prayer group that was started in Lexington, Jackson wrote:

This prayer meeting may be the means of accomplishing more than an army. I wish that such existed everywhere. How it does cheer my heart, to hear God's people praying for our cause, and for me! I greatly praise the prayers of the pious. [111]

The general sent many letters to his minister in Lexington, Reverend White. Jackson often ended his messages in this manner:

And now, present me affectionately to all my friends and brethren, and say to them, the greatest kindness they can show me is to pray for me. [112]

On June 20, 1862, at Gordonsville he wrote these lines to Mrs. Jackson:

For your prayers accept my warmest thanks, and I trust that you, and all our Christian people will with increased unrestling with God implore His blessing upon our cause. He can give us victory, and crown us with complete success, and He alone can. My trust is in Him, and in Him alone; and unto His name be all the glory for every success and every blessing. [113]

Again Jackson sent these rather pointed lines to his lovely companion:

If we were only that obedient people that we should be, I should, with increased confidence, look for a speedy termination of hostilities. Let us pray more and live more to the glory of God.[114]

Later in the war Jackson began to connect prayer with peace. He wrote, "I trust, that in answer to the prayers of *God's people*, He will soon give us peace."[115] Again the general expressed himself about the same connection:

I hope to have the privilege of joining in prayer for peace at the time you name, and hope that all our Christian people will; but peace should not be the chief object of prayer in our country. It should aim more specially at imploring God's forgiveness of our sins, and praying that He will make our people a holy people. If we are but His, all things shall work together for the good of our country, and no good thing He will withhold from it.[116]

There is no doubt that Jackson felt he was an instrument in the hand of God. Much of his correspondence referred directly to this belief. After First Manassas, he wrote:

My preservation was entirely due, as was the glorious victory, to our God, to whom be all the glory, honor and praise. Whilst great credit is due to other parts of our gallant army, God made my brigade more instrumental than any other in repulsing the main attack.[117]

Following another battle Jackson sent this message to his wife:

Our movement yesterday was a great success; I think the most successful military movement of my life. But I expect to receive far more credit for it than I deserve. Most men will think I had planned it all from the first; but it was not so—I simply took advantage of circumstances as they were presented to me in the providence of God. I feel that His hand led me: let us give Him all the glory.[118]

The general wrote, on November 4, 1861:

I shall have a great labor to perform, but through the blessing of an ever-kind [sic] Heavenly Father, I trust that He will enable me and other instrumentalities to accomplish it.[119]

At Harpers Ferry, Jackson expressed himself to his wife in this manner:

I am thankful to say that an ever-kind [sic] Providence, who causes "all things to work together for good to them that love Him," has given me the post which I prefer above all others, and has given me an independent command. To His name be all the praise.[120]

There are some other messages written by the commander that offer further insight into the depth of his Christian character. He enjoyed attending church and used these lines to describe some meetings:

Yesterday I heard Doctor M.A. Hoge preach in his church, and also in the camp of the Stonewall Brigade. It is a great comfort to have the privilege of spending a quiet Sabbath, within the walls of a house dedicated to the service of God.[121]

When Mrs. Jackson became discouraged on one occasion, the general wrote these lines to her:

So live that your suffering may be sanctified to you; remembering that our light afflictions, which are but for a moment, work out for us a few more exceeding and eternal weight of glory.[122]

The general worked as if everything depended upon himself and prayed as if everything depended upon his Father in Heaven. He sent this message to his wife, which offers insight about his conduct:

> You must not expect to hear from me very often as I expect to have more work than I have ever had, in the same length of time, before; but don't be concerned about me, as an ever-kind [sic] Heavenly Father will give me all needful aid.[123]

Finally, and perhaps most importantly, it should be remembered that this Christian man, who served in the profession of arms, hated war. Most soldiers who feel the terror of the battlefield, who see their brothers torn to shreds by enemy bullets, who hear the cry of the wounded, have a strong distaste for this necessary evil. Jackson was no exception. Near the end of 1862 he wrote to his wife: "I hope that the war will soon be over, and that I shall never again have to take the field."[124]

DEATH

Jackson went to sleep with his staff on a cool evening in 1863. The general had no covering, so his aide-de-camp, Lieutenant Smith, gave him a cape. At first he would not take it, but with persistence on the part of the lieutenant, the commander accepted. A few hours later, after nearly everyone was asleep, Jackson got up and put the cape over the young staff officer. The night was cool, and the next morning the general woke up with a bad cold. The illness did not slow him down, but it did foreshadow his death.[125]

Southern units at the front of Jackson's line near Chancellorsville on May 2 reported that Union troops were converging and appeared to be preparing for an attack. The commander decided to conduct a reconnaissance of the area with some of the members of his staff. So in the company of Captains

J.K. Boswell, Joseph Morrison and R.E. Wilbourn, Jackson rode toward the front.[126] The object of the mission was accomplished, and it was found that the Northern general, Joseph Hooker, was preparing his army for battle.[127]

The Confederate troops on the front lines were not warned sufficiently that a reconnaissance mission was taking place. While the general and his aids were making their return, they suddenly heard a shout, "Yankee cavalry!"[128] and a loud volley. The fire was directed at the commander's party, and many of the men were either killed or wounded by their own troops. In this freak accident, Jackson received wounds in the left arm and wrist.[129]

The general's horse, Little Sorrel, was terribly excited by the shooting, and so Jackson's problems did not end with the fire. At first, the animal ran toward the enemy, but the commander was able to turn it around with his wounded hand. Then Little Sorrel ran toward the Southern troops and took Jackson under a small tree. The general was knocked in the head by some limbs and his face was cut badly. Finally, the horse was halted by Captain Wilbour, and the general fell into the young officer's arms.[130]

Jackson was lying on the ground while the soldiers were preparing to carry him back behind the lines, when the Union artillery started to fire on them. This made the event even more chaotic.[131] In a few minutes the general began his journey to the rear.[132] His last official order before leaving the field was, "General Pender, you must keep your men together and hold your ground."[133] As the men carried Jackson through the lines, many of the troops wondered who it was. The party was asked so many times that the commander said, "When asked, just say it is a Confederate officer."[134] Jackson did not want his troops to lose their morale with the news of his misfortune.

General Jackson was taken to Dr. Hunter McGuire as

soon as possible, and medical attention was given. The doctor said, "I hope you are not badly hurt, General?" Jackson replied weakly, "I am badly injured, doctor. I fear I am dying." Then after a short pause the general said, "I am glad you have come. I think the wound in my shoulder is still bleeding."[135] While the medical officer was checking Jackson, the commander sent Lieutenant Morrison to escort Mrs. Jackson from Richmond.[136] It did not take long for the doctor to conclude that the general's left arm should be amputated. When he asked Jackson about this possible course of action, the soldier replied, "Yes, certainly! Dr. McGuire, do for me whatever you think right."[137] The arm was soon removed. General Lee sent a message to Jackson as soon as he learned of the accident. Lee said:

> Give him my affectionate regards, and tell him to make haste and get well, and come back to me as soon as he can. He has lost his left arm but I have lost my right arm.[138]

General Lee sent another note to his wounded subordinate. He told Jackson that his recovery position in the wilderness was too close to Union lines and that he should travel at once to Guinea's Station, which was much farther in the rear.[139] Jackson immediately complied with the request and started on his trip in a medical wagon. The general seemed to enjoy the travel and conversed a great deal with the drivers and guards.[140] However, he would not talk about his wounds unless someone asked about them.[141] The trip did not take long, and Jackson was soon at Guinea's Station with his wife and daughter, Julia.[142]

When the commander arrived at Guinea's Station he gave Mrs. Jackson a message that General Lee had sent to him earlier. Lee had written:

> General: I have just received your note informing me that you were wounded. I cannot express my regret at the occurrence.

Could I have directed events, I should have chosen, for the
good of the country, to have been disabled in your stead. I
congratulate you upon the victory which is due to your skill
and energy.[143]

After his wife finished reading the note, Jackson said, "General
Lee is very kind: [*sic*] but he should give the glory to God."[144]

The General requested that his chaplain, Mr. B.T. Lacy,
see him every day at ten o'clock for the purpose of scripture
study and prayer.[145] The first time the minister saw Jackson
at Guinea's Station he remarked, "Oh, General, what a calamity!" The commander replied:

You see me severely wounded, but not depressed—not un-
happy. I believe it has been done according to God's holy will,
and I acquiesce entirely in it. You may think it strange; but
you never saw me more perfectly contented than I am to-day;
for I am sure that my Heavenly Father designs this affliction
for my good. I am perfectly satisfied that either in this life, or
in that which is to come, I shall discover that what is now
regarded as a calamity is a blessing. I can wait until God, in
his own time, shall make known to me the object He has in
thus afflicting me. But why should I not rather rejoice in it as
a blessing, and not look on it as a calamity at all? If it were in
my power to replace my arm, I would not dare do it unless I
could know that it was the will of my Heavenly Father.[146]

Later the general went on to say "Many people would regard
this as a great misfortune. I regard it as one of the great
blessings of my life." Then an aide in the room said, "All things
work together for the good to those that love God." Jackson
remarked, "Yes, yes! That's it."[147]

On Monday, May 4, 1863, Jackson's physical condition
seemed to be quite well, even improving.[148] That night he
slept calmly and recovered from the shock of his amputated
arm.[149] However, after Monday the general's health became

increasingly worse. His pain grew more intense, and many of his conversations with other officers had to be discontinued to conserve strength.[150] The cold the Jackson had a few nights earlier was rapidly turning into pneumonia, and he was so exhausted from his duties that he could not fight off the disease. By Thursday night, the commander was suffering from a severe case of nausea. He asked his servant, Jim, to place a warm, damp cloth on his chest; this helped somewhat.[151]

The main physician, Dr. S.B. Morrison, knew by Friday that the general would not recover.[152] On Saturday, Jackson wanted to see Chaplain Lacy, but it was so hard for the soldier to breathe that he could not speak with the minister.[153] An attempt was made to revive his body processes by giving him some brandy and water. The commander found its taste extremely abhorrent and replied, "It tastes like fire, and cannot do me any good."[154] Later Chaplain Lacy could see that the end was near, and he requested to stay with Jackson rather than leave to preach to the troops on Sunday. The request was denied by the general; he would not forget his men.[155]

It was evident by Sunday morning that Jackson had only a few more hours to live.[156] He had always wanted to die on the Sabbath, and now his desire was coming true.[157] The doctor informed Mrs. Jackson that she could tell her husband about his condition. After she completed her sad news, the general was quiet for a moment and then said, "It will be infinite gain to be translated to heaven."[158] Later, after thinking about death for some time, Jackson exclaimed, "Very good, very good; it is all right!"[159]

The commander's wife wanted to know his last desires, so she posed some questions. She asked if he thought the spirit of the Savior was present with him. His simple reply was, "Yes."[160] Next, Mrs. Jackson wondered if she and Julia should live with her father. The general said: "Yes, you have a kind and good father; but no one is so kind and good as your heavenly father."[161] Finally, she asked where he wanted to be buried. Jackson did not answer this question. After a short time his wife said she thought Lexington would be a good place. The commander replied, "Yes, in Lexington."[162] However, there was some evident bitterness in his brief remark.[163]

Mrs. Jackson could not think of any more questions, so a lady brought Julia into the room. The soldier had lost much of his sight and he had little understanding of what was taking place; but when he saw his daughter, Jackson's face lit up with a smile. He said quietly, "Little darling! Sweet one!"[164] Julia was placed at his bedside and playfully enjoyed his caress for a few short minutes. Then the general lost all of the strength in his arm and slowly entered a state of unconsciousness.[165]

While Jackson was apparently sleeping, he said quite distinctly: "Let us pass over the river and rest under the shade of the trees."[166] His final words had thus been spoken. The doctor in the room thought the commander was gone, so he permitted Mrs. Jackson to grieve over her husband. She kissed him, as her tears were dripping over his pale face, and she cried, "Oh, doctor, cannot you do something more?"[167] These words of desperation brought Jackson back momentarily. He opened his eyes fully, looked up into her face, and then closed them forever.[168]

In Washington, D.C., on May 13, 1863, *The Daily Chronicle* printed an article by John Forney titled "The Death of Stonewall Jackson."[169] The author wrote:

Stonewall Jackson is dead. While we are only too glad to be rid, in any way, of so terrible a foe, our sense of relief is not unmingled with emotions of sorrow and sympathy at the death of so brave a man. Every man who possesses the least particle of magnanimity must admire the qualities for which Stonewall Jackson was celebrated—his heroism, his bravery, his sublime devotion, his purity of character . . . Stonewall Jackson was a great general, a grave soldier, a noble Christian and a pure man. May God throw these great virtues against the sins of the secessionists, the advocates of a great national crime.[170]

On the same day President Abraham Lincoln sent this message to Mr. Forney regarding the article: "I wish to lose no time in thanking you for the excellent and manly article in the *Chronicle* on 'Stonewall Jackson.' "[171]

NOTES

1. Jones, p. 86.
2. Jackson, *Memoirs*, p. 146.
3. Dabney, p. 250.
4. Ibid.
5. Jackson, *Memoirs*, p. 209.
6. Cooke, p. 68.
7. Ibid.
8. Casler, p. 26.
9. Ibid.
10. Dabney, p. 273.
11. Ibid. p. 276.
12. Douglas, p. 25.
13. Jackson, *Memoirs*, p. 229.
14. Ibid. p. 234.
15. Ibid. p. 235.
16. Cooke, p. 346.
17. Ibid. p. 274.
18. Ibid.
19. Jackson, *Memoirs*, p. 318.
20. Ibid. p. 317.
21. Casler, p. 154.
22. Cooke, p. 220.
23. Ibid. p. 89.
24. Douglas, p. 71.
25. Cooke, p. 248.
26. Dabney, p. 110.
27. Douglas, p.55.

28. Ibid. p. 110.
29. Ibid.
30. Cooke, p. 144.
31. Ibid. p. 185.
32. Douglas, p. 39.
33. Cooke, p. 199.
34. Ibid. p. 197.
35. Ibid. p. 86.
36. Jackson, *Memoirs*, p. 226.
37. Douglas, p. 155.
38. Ibid.
39. Ibid. p. 20.
40. Ibid. p. 67.
41. Ibid. p. 68.
42. Jackson, *Memoirs*, p. 155.
43. Douglas, p. 98.
44. Cooke, p. 200.
45. Ibid. pp. 362–363.
46. Casler, p. 68.
47. Dabney, p. 81.
48. Ibid. p. 191.
49. Casler, p. 92.
50. Dabney, pp. 229–230.
51. Ibid. p. 589.
52. Ibid. p. 635.
53. Jackson, *Memoirs*, p. 183.
54. Ibid. p. 187.
55. Ibid. p. 191.
56. Ibid. pp. 183–184.
57. Douglas, p. 108.
58. Jones, p. 97.
59. Ibid.
60. Ibid.
61. Cooke, p. 393.
62. Jones, p. 89.
63. Ibid.
64. Jackson, *Memoirs*, p. 302.
65. Douglas, p. 36.
66. Cooke, p. 325.
67. Jones, p. 87.
68. Ibid.
69. Ibid. p. 93.
70. Ibid.
71. Douglas, p. 19.

72. Jones, p. 92.
73. Ibid.
74. Jackson, *Memoirs*, pp. 444–446.
75. Ibid.
76. Douglas, pp. 92–93.
77. Jones, p. 251.
78. Cooke, p. 274.
79. Jones, p. 251.
80. Jones, p. 93.
81. Ibid.
82. Ibid. pp. 96–97.
83. Ibid.
84. Ibid. pp. 93–94.
85. Ibid. p. 96.
86. Ibid.
87. Dabney, p. 646.
88. Jackson, *Memoirs,* p. 385.
89. Jones, p. 83.
90. Jackson, *Life and Letters,* p. 287.
91. Dabney, p. 652.
92. Ibid. p. 653.
93. Ibid.
94. Ibid. p. 649.
95. Ibid. pp. 649–650.
96. Jackson, *Memoirs*, p. 389.
97. Dabney, p. 656.
98. Arnold, p. 337.
99. Dabney, p. 251.
100. Douglas, p. 94.
101. Ibid.
102. Ibid.
103. Cooke, p. 135.
104. Dabney, p. 353.
105. Jones, pp. 91–92.
106. Jackson, *Memoirs*, p. 177.
107. Dabney, p. 537.
108. Ibid. p. 656.
109. Ibid. p. 644.
110. Ibid. p. 329.
111. Ibid. pp. 635–636.
112. Ibid. p. 107.
113. Howard Mcknight Wilson, *Records of Lexington Presbytery* (Lexington: Lexington Presbytery Centennial Committee, 1960), p. 6.
114. Dabney, p. 641.

115. Ibid. p. 141.
116. Ibid.
117. Ibid. p. 329.
118. Jones, p. 98.
119. Dabney, p. 248.
120. Ibid. p. 185.
121. Ibid., p. 489.
122. Ibid. p. 329.
123. Ibid. p. 185.
124. Ibid. p. 330.
125. Douglas, p. 220.
126. Ibid. p. 222.
127. Jackson, *Memoirs*, p. 426.
128. Douglas, p. 222
129. Ibid.
130. Ibid. pp. 122–123.
131. Ibid.
132. Cooke, p. 425.
133. Casler, p. 154.
134. Cooke, p. 425.
135. Jackson, *Memoirs*, p. 433.
136. Dabney, p. 707.
137. Cooke, p. 439.
138. Jackson, *Memoirs*, p. 454.
139. Dabney, p. 711.
140. Cooke, p. 441.
141. Ibid. p. 440.
142. Douglas, p. 229.
143. Jones, p. 98.
144. Ibid.
145. Jackson, *Memoirs*, p. 444.
146. Jones, pp. 90–91.
147. Cooke, p. 442.
148. Dabney, p. 713.
149. Cooke, p. 442.
150. Dabney, p. 715.
151. Jackson, *Memoirs*, p. 440.
152. Dabney, p. 719.
153. Jackson, *Memoirs*, p. 453.
154. Ibid. p. 454.
155. Ibid. p. 453.
156. Cooke, p. 443.
157. Jackson, *Memoirs*, p. 453.
158. Jones, p. 100.
159. Ibid.

160. Dabney, pp. 722–724.
161. Ibid.
162. Ibid.
163. Ibid.
164. Jackson, *Memoirs,* p. 456.
165. Dabney, pp. 722–724.
166. Ibid.
167. Ibid.
168. Ibid.
169. Roy Bird Cook, *The Family and Early Life of Stonewall Jackson* (Charleston: Charleston Printing Company, 1948), pp 170–172.
170. Ibid.
171. Ibid.

CHAPTER SEVEN

Conclusion

All things work together for the good of those that love God.

Thomas J. Jackson

There are many conclusions that can be made from this study of Thomas Jonathan Jackson. During his boyhood, he was no stranger to trials. Thomas's positive reaction to this early adversity set a pattern for his entire life.[1] The young man also developed an extremely independent attitude. He sought the position of constable in order to earn his own way.[2] Later in his youth it was evident that he had an ability to set priorities. Thomas turned down a tour of Washington, D.C., so that he could travel to West Point as soon as possible.[3]

Jackson continued to mold his character as a cadet at West Point. Some traits were easier to form than others. The young man from Virginia found it difficult to control his temper, and this came to light in his experience with the stolen rifle.[4] Jackson gained an obsession for self-improvement that lasted throughout his life. This was best exemplified by the ethical code that he compiled.[5] The country boy brought an inferiority complex with him to the Academy.[6] This attitude caused him to work excessively and resulted in the reoccurrence of his dyspepsia condition.[7]

Some important aspects are learned about the artillery officer while he served in the United States Army. Jackson was an insecure person because of the early loss of his parents. This gap in his life was partially filled by Colonel Frank Taylor. The senior officer had a dominant, fatherly instinct and that was exactly what the young West Pointer needed.[8] Jackson was also an egotistical person. His rapid promotion in Mexico was, to a large extent, the result of his strong desire and hard work for recognition.[9] The officer's letters during this time reveal the fact that even he recognized this personality trait.[10]

The major's experience in Lexington foreshadowed much of his conduct in the Civil War. He was a quiet man and this reflected his basic dislike for people.[11] Jackson had been socially mistreated too many times; this prevented him from trusting anyone.[12] When he had a conversation with an associate, the odd professor spoke in a submissive tone. However, this outward expression hid the true character of a very determined man.[13] Jackson should not be stereotyped with a singular personality because he was a dynamic individual. The account of his activities at home demonstrate how different he could be.[14] Also, the major did not let poor health inhibit his progress. Rather than despairing over his weak eyes, he used this condition to develop his memory.[15] Jackson turned to religion for strength in overcoming his physical condition.[16] This attitude might appear to be an exceedingly dependent means to some people, but none can dispute the positive result. Much of the professor's Christian philosophy came from Reverend William S. White. The two men were always close and profited from each other's friendship.[17] Although Jackson owned slaves, it is evident that he did not approve of the institution. The major recognized his inability to change the Southern way of life; so he initiated activities, such as the black Sunday school, to improve the condition of the suppressed race.[18]

The general's personality in the Confederate Army was, in a broad sense, simply an extension of the peculiar professor from Lexington. His large beard tended to hide the fact that Jackson was a young man. At his death he was only 39. The commander's nickname, Stonewall, is also associated with misconception and must be considered a misnomer. During the war, no army was more maneuverable than Jackson's "foot cavalry."[19] The general's successful Valley Campaign was a classic example of the mobile concept of warfare in action.[20] However, two important factors must be remembered with reference to these battles. First, Jackson fought near his own home, and naturally he knew the topography well. Second, he employed a defensive strategy, which automatically increased his strength for combat about three times what it normally would be. It should be recognized that the commander had a far greater love for his home state of Virginia than he did for the Confederacy. It was the doctrine of state's rights that led him to fight for the South.[21] During the general's service in the Confederate Army, he continually placed duty above self. Perhaps the best example of this was the experience that Jackson had with Loring.[22] The commander also thought of himself as a Christian rather than a Presbyterian. This is reflected in his many letters concerning Christianity and in his indifference about the denomination of his chaplains.[23] Perhaps most importantly, Jackson developed a strong belief that he was an instrument in God's hand. This conviction led him to write one day on the battlefield, "God blessed our arms with victory. . . ."[24]

NOTES

1. Henderson, p. 11.
2. Jackson, *Memoirs*, pp. 27–28.
3. Ibid. p. 32.
4. Henderson, p. 19.
5. Jackson, *Memoirs*, pp. 35–37.
6. Tate, pp. 29–39.
7. Henderson, p. 21.
8. Ibid. pp. 52–53.
9. Ibid. p. 46.
10. Arnold, p. 91.
11. Jackson, *Memoirs*, p. 63.
12. Ibid. p. 65.
13. Henderson, p. 63.
14. Ibid. p. 65.
15. Arnold, p. 153.
16. Jackson, *Memoirs*, p. 363.
17. Ibid. p. 59.
18. Jones, p. 85.
19. Cooke, p. 274.
20. Douglas, pp. 92–93.
21. Jackson, *Memoirs*, p. 139.
22. Ibid. p. 229.
23. Dabney, p. 141.
24. Cook, p. 167.

Bibliography

PRIMARY SOURCES

Allan, Elizabeth Preston. *The Life and Letters of Margaret Junkin Preston*. Boston and New York: Houghton Mifflin and Company, 1903.

Arnold, Thomas Jackson. *Early Life and Letters of General Thomas J. Jackson*. Richmond: Fleming H. Revell Company, 1916.

Casler, John O. *Four Years in the Stonewall Brigade*. Dayton: Morningside Bookshop, 1971.

Cooke, John Esten. Stonewall Jackson: *A Military Biography*. New York: D. Appleton and Company, 1876.

Dabney, R.L. *Life and Campaigns of Lieut.- Gen. Thomas J. Jackson*. New York: Blebock and Company, 1866.

————. Papers. Richmond: the Library, Union Theological Seminary, 1898. Microfilm, sections a, b, c, d.

Douglas, Henry Kyd. *I Rode with Stonewall*. Chapel Hill: The University of North Carolina Press, 1940.

Jackson, Mary Anna. *Life and Letters of General Thomas J. Jackson*. New York: Harper and Brothers, 1891.

————. *Memoirs of Stonewall Jackson*. Louisville: The Prentice Press, 1895.

Jackson, Thomas Jonathan. Personal Letters, Military Correspondence and Reports. Special Collections, Preston Library, Virginia Military Institute, Lexington, Virginia.

Jones, J. William. *Christ in the Camp*. Atlanta: The Martin and Hoyt Company, 1887.

―――. "The Inner Life of 'Stonewall' Jackson," *Highways and Byways*, no date available, pp. 8–14.

―――. "Stonewall Jackson," *Southern Historical Papers*, no date available, pp. 145–175.

Junkin, P.X. *George Junkin*. Philadelphia: Lippincott and Company, 1871.

Lee, Susan P. *Memoirs of William Nelson Pendleton*. Philadelphia: Lippincott and Company, 1893.

McCormic Library. Franklin Society Records. Lexington, Virginia: Washington and Lee University, no date available.

Moore, Edward A. *The Story of a Cannoneer under Stonewall Jackson*. New York and Washington: The Neale Publishing Company, 1907.

Presbyterian Church, Minutes and Records. Lexington, Virginia: Lexington Presbyterian Church, no date available.

Smith, R.M. *Reports of Battles, Richmond*. Richmond: published by order of Congress (Confederate), 1864.

United States Military Academy. Thomas J. Jackson's Academic Record while a Cadet at the United States Military Academy. West Point: United States Army, no date available.

White, H.M. *Rev. William S. White*. Richmond: Presbyterian Committee of Publication, 1891.

White, William S. *The Gospel Ministry, in a Series of Letters from a Father to his Sons*. Philadelphia: Presbyterian Board of publication, 1860.

―――. Papers, Sunday School Lessons. Special Collections, McCormic Library, Washington and Lee University, Lexington, Virginia.

SECONDARY SOURCES

Catton, Bruce. *This Hallowed Ground*. New York: Pocket Books, 1965.

————. *The Centennial History of the Civil War*. Garden City, New York: Doubleday, 1961.

Chambers, Lenior. *Stonewall Jackson*. New York: W. Morrow, 1959.

Cole, Arthur Charles. *The Irrepressible Conflict*. New York: The Macmillan Company, 1934.

Commanger, Henry Steel. *The Blue and the Gray*. Indianapolis: Bobbs-Merrill, 1950.

Cook, Roy Bird. *The Family and Early Life of Stonewall Jackson*. Charleston: Charleston Printing Company, 1948.

Couper, William. *One Hundred Years of Virginia Military Institute*. Richmond: Garrett and Massie Company, 1939.

Davis, Burke. *They Called Him Stonewall*. New York: Holt, Rinehart and Winston, Inc., 1961.

Eaton, Clement. *A History of the Southern Confederacy*. New York: The Free Press, 1954.

Freeman, Douglas Southhall. *Lee's Lieutenants*. New York: C. Scribner's Sons, 1944.

Henderson, G.R.F. *Stonewall Jackson and the American Civil War*. New York: Longmans, Green and Company, 2 vols., 1919.

Johnson, Thomas C. *A History of the Southern Presbyterian Church*. New York: The Christian Literature Company, 1894.

Long, Andrew Davidson. *Stonewall's "Foot Cavalrymen."* United States: Walter E. Long, 1965.

O'Connor, Thomas H. *The Disunited States*. New York: Dodd, Mead and Company, 1972.

Offill, Paul Miller Jr. "Stonewall Jackson: a Case Study in Religious Motivation and its effect on Confederate Leadership and Morale." Unpublished Master's thesis, University of Pittsburgh, 1961.

Richards, Warren J. "God Blessed Our Arms With Victory." Unpublished Master's thesis, Utah State University, 1974.

Roland, Charles P. *The Confederacy*. Chicago and London: The University of Chicago Press, 1972.

Silver, James W. *Confederate Morale and Church Propaganda*. Tuscaloosa, Alabama: Confederate Publishing Company, Inc., 1957.

Smyth, Ellison A. "A History of Presbyterianism in Rockbridge County Virginia." Unpublished Master's thesis, Washington and Lee University, 1938.

Sweet, William Warren. *Revivalism in America*. New York: Charles Scribner's Sons, 1944.

————.*The Presbyterians, a Collection of Source Material*. New York: Couper Square, 1964.

Tate, Allen. *Stonewall Jackson*. New York: G.P. Putnam's Sons, 1956.

Tompson, Ernest Trice. *Presbyterians in the South*. Richmond: John Knox Press, 1963.

VanDiver, Frank E. *Mighty Stonewall*. New York: McGraw-Hill Book Company, Inc., 1957.

————. *Their Tattered Flags*. New York: Harper and Row, 1970.

Wiley, Bell Irvin. *The Life of Jonney Reb*. New York: Charter Books, 1962.

Wilson, Howard McKnight. *Records of Lexington Presbytery*. Lexington, Virginia: Lexington Presbyterian Centennial Committee, 1960.

ARTICLES

Chambers, Lenoir. "The Whole Jackson," The Virginia Civil War Commission, May 1, 1963, pp. 3–13.

Couper, William. "War and Work," The Rockbridge Historical Society, April 22, 1940, pp. 3–11.

Malone, Dumas. "Thomas Jonathan Jackson," *Dictionary of American Biography*, 1932, pp. 556–559.

McCorkle, Henry L. "Stonewall—A 'Rare and Eminent Christian,' " *Presbyterian Life*, May 29, 1954, pp. 1–6.

Murry, Joseph James. History of the Lexington Presbyterian Church. Unpublished. 1963. pp. 1–6.

———. "The Religious Life of Stonewall Jackson," no publication, 1963, pp. 1–8.

Semple, Henry Churchill. "The Spirituality of Stonewall Jackson and Catholic Influences," *Catholic World*, 1922–23, pp. 349–356.

"Southwest Corner Articles tell of Jackson's Church Activities." 1948. Rockbridge County News, July 15.